The Green New Deal

Economics and Policy Analytics

Benjamin Zycher

April 2019

AMERICAN ENTERPRISE INSTITUTE

ISBN-13: 978-0-8447-5022-4 (paperback)
ISBN-13: 978-0-8447-5023-1 (ebook)

American Enterprise Institute
1789 Massachusetts Avenue, NW
Washington, DC 20036
www.aei.org

The American Enterprise Institute (AEI) is a nonpartisan, nonprofit, 501(c)(3) educational organization and does not take institutional positions on any issues. The views expressed here are those of the author(s).

Contents

Executive Summary

The Green New Deal (GND) is a set of policy proposals, some more concrete than others, with the central advertised goal of ameliorating a purported climate crisis by implementing policies that would reduce US greenhouse gas (GHG) emissions to zero, or to "net zero," by 2050 in some formulations. In addition, the GND incorporates other important social-policy goals as a means of forging a majority political coalition in support.

The GND's central premise is that such policies—either despite or by reducing sharply the economic value of some substantial part of the US resource base and the energy-producing and energy-consuming capital stock—would increase the size of the economy in real terms, increase employment, improve environmental quality, and improve distributional equity. That is a "broken windows" argument: The destruction of resources increases aggregate wealth. It is not to be taken seriously.

Moreover, notwithstanding the assertions from GND proponents that it is an essential policy to confront purportedly adverse climate phenomena, the future temperature impacts of the zero-emissions objective would be barely distinguishable from zero: 0.173°C by 2100, under the maximum Intergovernmental Panel on Climate Change parameter (equilibrium climate sensitivity) about the effects of reduced GHG emissions. Under an assumption consistent with the findings reported in the recent peer-reviewed literature, the effect would be 0.083°C by 2100, a policy impact not measurable against normal variation in temperatures. This conclusion is not controversial and suggests strongly that the GND's real goal is wealth redistribution to favored political interests under the GND social-policy agenda and a dramatic increase in government control of resource allocation more generally.

A GND policy would yield no benefits in its central energy, environment, and climate context, but it would impose large economic costs. Simple correlations among variables do not demonstrate causation, but the historical data on energy consumption and production, growth in gross domestic product, employment, rising incomes and energy consumption, and poverty make it clear that the GND would yield large adverse effects in each of those dimensions. In particular, because rising incomes result in greater energy demands and because the GND intellectual framework views conventional energy as a social "bad," parameters that increase individual and national incomes—such as education and health investment, technological advances, and investments in productive plant and equipment—also must be viewed in a negative light. Accordingly, one logical corollary to the GND policy agenda is a reduction in such direct or indirect investments in human capital. Thus does the GND reveal the essential antihuman core of the modern opposition to conventional energy.

The electricity component of the GND is the least ambiguous. A highly conservative estimate of the aggregate cost of that set of policies alone would be $490.5 billion per year, permanently, or $3,845 per year per household, an impact that would vary considerably across the states if the GND were financed through electricity rates rather than the federal budget. Under such a ratepayer finance assumption, the lowest household cost of $222 per year would be observed in Vermont. The highest would be observed in Wyoming: $17,103 per household per year.

The GND electricity mandate would create significant environmental damage—there is nothing clean about "clean" electricity—and require massive land use of over 115 million acres (about 180,000 square miles), about 15 percent larger than the land area of California.

Because of the need for conventional backup generation to avoid blackouts in a "100 percent renewable system" and because those backup units would have to be cycled up and down depending on wind and sunlight conditions, one ironic effect would be GHG emissions from natural gas–fired backup generation 22 percent *higher* than those resulting in 2017 from all natural gas–fired power generation. And those backup emissions would be over 35 percent of the emissions from all power generation in 2017.

Without fossil-fired backup generation, the national and regional electricity systems would be characterized by a significant decline in service reliability—that is, a large increase in the frequency and duration of blackouts. Battery backup technology cannot solve this problem. It is unlikely that a power system characterized by regular, widespread service interruptions would be acceptable to a large majority of Americans. Accordingly, the emissions effects of backup generation as just described would in fact be observed, which is to say that to a significant degree the GND is self-defeating in its asserted climate goals. That is another reason to conclude that the true goals are an expansion of wealth transfers to favored interests and the power of government to command and allocate resources. Moreover, the reduction in individual and aggregate incomes attendant upon the GND policies would yield a reduction in the collective political willingness to invest in environmental protection over time.

As shown in Table ES1, the annual economic cost of the GND would be about $9 trillion. These figures exclude the costs of the massive shifts in the transportation sector mandated by the GND, the building retrofit objectives, high-speed rail, and other policies. Those components of the GND are far more ambiguous than the electricity dimension and thus lend themselves less to a rigorous cost analysis. The figures also exclude many of the economic costs of the adverse environmental effects of the GND electricity mandate and the costs of the inexorable increase in government authoritarianism attendant upon the GND, an effect difficult to measure but very real nonetheless.

The claim from some GND supporters, based on a set of arguments subsumed under the heading Modern Monetary Theory, that it can be financed with money creation is deeply dubious. The use of money creation to finance the GND means that the resulting inflation would be fully anticipated, so that the inflation would constitute an explicit tax on currency, with a substantial set of such adverse consequences as a degradation of the currency as a store of value, adverse behavioral responses by holders of currency, and the like. The use of money creation as an instrument to service debt incurred to finance

Table ES1. Annual Costs of the Green New Deal (Billions of 2018 Dollars)

GND Policy	Cost	Total Cost
Renewable Electricity Mandate		490
New Renewable Power Capacity	357	
Backup Capacity, Generation	76.9	
Emissions from Backup Generation	30.8	
Transmission	18	
Land	7.8	
Budget Cost of Forging a GND Political Coalition		4,000
Excess Burden of the Tax System		4,460
Annual Total		**8,950**

Source: Tables 10 and 11.

the GND also is deeply dubious, as any such approach would be based on an assumption that purchasers of government debt instruments would deliver real resources to the government with no expectation of receiving repayment in an equivalent amount of real resources plus interest. Lenders to the government are not so myopic. Moreover, the use of inflation as a mechanism for the acquisition of real resources for the government imposes its own set of large costs; the literature suggests that annual inflation rates of 10 percent or 20 percent would impose economic losses of about $2 trillion and $4 trillion per year, respectively. This effect is crudely analogous to the excess burden of the explicit tax system. Modern Monetary Theory is little more than the latest example of the old argument that there is available a free lunch, as illustrated by the argument from a prominent proponent that "anything that is technically feasible is financially affordable."

The GND represents a massive erosion in the ability of individuals and businesses to use their resources in ways that they deem appropriate. As the adverse consequences of the GND emerge and grow, it is inevitable that government will attempt to circumvent them by increasing explicit rationing and politicizing energy use, a process that inexorably will expand government surveillance of energy use and erode individual freedom and privacy. That has been the recent experience in California in the face of perceived water shortages.

Thus would the GND lead inexorably toward an expansion of authoritarianism under American government institutions. The GND proposals for the transportation sector would create large wealth transfers from rural, exurban, and suburban regions to urban ones, and they would reduce individual mobility sharply by increasing the government's ability to control transportation patterns.

The expansion of employment under the GND—in particular, the expansion of "green" employment—will prove illusory. The resource "sustainability" rationale for the GND is fundamentally incorrect analytically. Future generations rationally would vote in favor of policies maximizing the value of the capital stock to be bequeathed to them; policies engendering massive resource waste by the current generation are inconsistent with that goal. The current body of evidence on climate phenomena supports the hypothesis that some part of ongoing temperature trends and climate phenomena are anthropogenic in origin, but it does not support the argument that a climate crisis is present or looming. And the experience of Ontario under its Green Energy Act should give pause to policymakers considering the GND policy proposals.

The GND at its core is the substitution of central planning in place of market forces for resource allocation in the US energy and transportation sectors narrowly and in the broad industrial, commercial, and residential sectors writ large. Given the tragic and predictable record of central planning outcomes worldwide over the past century, the GND should be rejected.

1

Introduction: What Is the Objective of the Green New Deal?

With the new Democratic majority in the House of Representatives, it is unsurprising that legislative proposals and priorities in that body have changed from those promoted by the prior Republican majority. Prominent among the new proposals now being discussed and developed is the Green New Deal (GND).[1] Its multiple goals are broad, but in the official resolution they are driven by a central focus on climate policy.

[G]lobal temperatures must be kept below 1.5 degrees Celsius above preindustrialized levels to avoid the most severe impacts of a changing climate, which will require—

(A) global reductions in greenhouse gas emissions from human sources of 40 to 60 percent from 2010 levels by 2030; and

(B) net zero global emissions by 2050.

And "it is the duty of the Federal Government to create a Green New Deal," the goals of which "should be accomplished through a 10-year national mobilization . . . that will require the following goals and projects—"

- "Eliminating pollution and greenhouse gas emissions as much as technologically feasible";

- "Meeting 100 percent of the power demand in the United States through clean, renewable, and zero-emission energy sources . . . by dramatically expanding and upgrading renewable power sources";

- "Building or upgrading to energy-efficient, distributed, and 'smart' power grids";

- "Upgrading all existing buildings in the United States and building new buildings to achieve maximum energy efficiency";

- "Removing pollution and greenhouse gas emissions from manufacturing and industry as much as is technologically feasible";

- "Remov[ing] pollution and greenhouse gas emissions from the agricultural sector as much as is technologically feasible."

- "Overhauling transportation systems in the United States to remove pollution and greenhouse gas emissions from the transportation sector as much as is technologically feasible, through investment in . . . zero-emission vehicle infrastructure and manufacturing; clean, affordable, and accessible public transit, and high-speed rail."

Accordingly, the specific central policy objective of the GND is a reduction of US greenhouse gas (GHG) net emissions to zero by 2050, advocated as an ostensible solution to a purported climate crisis.[2] The zero "net emissions" goal implicitly must incorporate carbon capture and sequestration technologies and efforts to remove carbon dioxide from the atmosphere.[3] Neither has been shown to be feasible.[4]

Among the policy documents, analyses, frequently asked questions (FAQs) lists, and related materials available publicly in support of the GND, one searches in vain for an estimate of the temperature effect, say, in 2100, of a reduction of US GHG emissions to zero. If we apply the Environmental Protection Agency (EPA) climate model[5] to that straightforward question, under a 4.5°C assumption about the equilibrium climate sensitivity (ECS) of the climate system, thus magnifying the effects of reduced atmospheric concentrations of GHG,[6] the temperature effect would be 0.173°C. That impact would be difficult to measure, as it is barely greater than the standard deviation (0.11°C) of the surface (land-ocean) temperature record.[7] The midpoint of the

Intergovernmental Panel on Climate Change (IPCC) "likely" range for ECS is 3°C; under that assumption, the temperature effect of the GND in 2100 would be 0.137°C. Assuming an ECS of 2°C—greater than the average finding reported in the recent peer-reviewed literature—the temperature effect in 2100 would be 0.104°C, less than the standard deviation of the surface temperature record and thus not measurable against normal background variation. If we assume an ECS of 1.5°C, the temperature effect in 2100 would be 0.083°C.

Note that the other asserted climate impacts of changing atmospheric concentrations of GHG—sea levels, cyclone frequencies and intensities, droughts, etc.—are correlated closely with the asserted temperature effects.[8] This question of the climate impacts of the GND, ostensibly its main policy goal, is so obviously central to GND policy proposals that the failure of its proponents even to discuss it is revealing, and the long-standing unwillingness more generally of the advocates of climate policies to address it is both striking and part of a pattern.[9]

What explains this? One possibility is that the climate impacts of the policy proposals are so small—even, or especially, using analytic tools that have not been questioned by the policy proponents—that the silence on this question is necessary politically because acknowledging the trivial prospective climate effects would reduce political support for the proposals substantially, both in Congress and among the electorate. But if that is the case, why promote such ineffectual policies at all, if indeed a purported climate crisis is the central motivation?[10] One typical answer is that US climate policies would position the US to lead a global effort, such as that reflected in the Conferences of the Parties (COP) to the United Nations Framework Convention on Climate Change (UNFCCC).[11] The House resolution notes:[12]

Whereas, because the United States has historically been responsible for a disproportionate amount of greenhouse gas emissions, having emitted 20 percent of global greenhouse gas emissions through 2014, and has a high technological capacity, the United States must take a leading role in reducing emissions through economic transformation.

But even at an international level—putting aside the issue of whether agreements to reduce GHG emissions, such as that made at the 21st COP in Paris in 2015, are meaningful—any agreement even remotely plausible would reduce GHG emissions by amounts yielding temperature effects ranging from small to trivial.[13] Is it the position of the GND proponents, given the experience and long-standing frustrations of the UNFCCC process, that agreements on global GHG emissions reductions radically stronger than the Paris agreement are achievable?

GND proponents claim and want others to believe that national wealth and employment would be increased, environmental quality enhanced, and distributional equity improved by policies destroying the economic value of a significant part of the national resource base and the energy-producing and energy-consuming capital stock. That is the "broken windows" fallacy: The destruction of resources increases national wealth. It is a vast understatement to say that those premises are deeply dubious; indeed, they are so problematic that it is easy to conclude that the actual objectives of the GND differ markedly from the stated ones.

That the GND proponents advocate strong "climate" policies even given the trivial climate effects of the attendant policy prescriptions suggests strongly that environmental ("climate") benefits are not the central goal of the proponents and indeed are irrelevant. Instead, the actual goals are more likely political and ideological. This initial observation is consistent with the GND proponents' stated objectives, which simultaneously are environmental, economic, and social. In addition to the objectives specified above in the House resolution, there also are these (a sampling) in the same document, to be achieved "through a 10-year national mobilization":

- Creation of "millions of good, high-wage jobs [and] prosperity and economic security for all people of the United States";

- "Invest[ment] in the infrastructure and industry of the United States";

- "A sustainable environment";

- "Promot[ion of] justice and equity [for] 'frontline and vulnerable communities'";

- "Building a more sustainable food system";

- "Restoring and protecting threatened, endangered, and fragile ecosystems [through projects] that enhance biodiversity";

- "Guaranteeing universal access to clean water";

- "Providing . . . high-quality education . . . to all people of the United States";

- A "guarantee [of] a job with a family-sustaining wage, adequate family and medical leave, paid vacations, and retirement security to all people of the United States";

- Strengthening of unionization rights and of "labor, workplace health and safety, antidiscrimination, and wage and hour standards"; and

- "Providing all people of the United States with—high-quality health care; affordable, safe, and adequate housing; economic security; and clean water, clean air, healthy and affordable food, and access to nature."

The relationships between these policy objectives and the central goal of net zero US GHG emissions, which as discussed would yield approximately zero climate effects, remain largely obscure, except perhaps as policies designed to ameliorate the short-run transitional (economic "structural") impacts of the policies. Accordingly, it is not difficult to conclude that the real goals of the GND are the ones just delineated, which reasonably can be categorized as social rather than environmental.[14]

Chapter 2 discusses the correlations among energy consumption and production on the one hand and employment, gross domestic product (GDP) growth, household incomes, poverty, and national wealth on the other. It discusses also the antihuman implications of the ideological opposition to fossil fuels. Chapter 3 discusses the adverse environmental implications of the GND renewable electricity mandate. Chapter 4 discusses the direct costs of the GND renewable electricity mandate. Chapter 5 discusses the large hidden costs of the GND, including a state-by-state summary of the costs of the GND renewable electricity mandates under the assumption that the costs would be borne by power consumers through electricity rate increases. Chapter 6 discusses the inexorable authoritarian implications of the GND, driven by its essential nature as an exercise in central planning, in terms of "smart grid" proposals, rising blackout costs, the necessarily politicized allocation of increasingly scarce energy goods and services, and an effort to eliminate GHG emissions from the transportation sector. Chapter 7 offers short discussions of several ancillary topics, while Chapter 8 presents some concluding observations.

2

The Antihuman Core of the Green New Deal: Energy, National Wealth, Employment, Poverty, and Investment in Human Capital

Regardless of the actual motivating economic and political objectives of the GND—alleviation of the purported climate crisis versus the social parameters listed above—the GND essentially is an effort to replace most conventional energy, particularly in the electric power and transportation sectors, with "renewable" energy. This must mean wind and solar power predominantly for the former and some sort of battery system for the latter. By imposing an artificial (i.e., policy-driven) constraint on the use of available resources and energy-producing and energy-consuming capital that otherwise would be economic to use, the GND by design would destroy the economic value (i.e., prevent the use) of some significant part of the national resource base and the capital stock.[15]

The proponents of the GND assert that this destruction of the economic value of resources and capital would increase national wealth and employment, improve environmental quality, and enhance distributional equity—a deeply dubious proposition. Accordingly, it is useful to examine the historical data on the broad relationships among energy consumption and production, economic conditions and aggregates, and several correlations, in particular for lower-income Americans.[16] (The implications for environmental quality are discussed in Chapter 3.) Many proponents of renewable and other forms of unconventional energy argue that fossil fuels no longer enjoy a cost advantage over unconventional energy technologies, an assertion inconsistent with the inability of renewable power to compete without large subsidies and guaranteed market shares.[17] Replacing lower-cost

Figure 1. Annual Percent Changes: Real GDP and Primary Energy Consumption

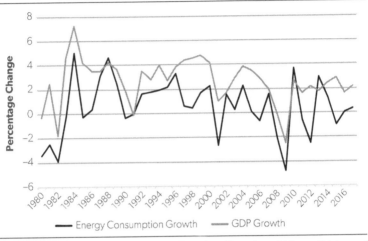

Energy Consumption Growth — GDP Growth

Source: US Energy Information Administration, Total Energy, https://www.eia.gov/totalenergy/data/browser/
index.php?tbl=T01.01#/?f=M; US Bureau of Economic Analysis, "Gross Domestic Product," https://www.
bea.gov/data/gdp/gross-domestic-product; and US Bureau of Economic Analysis, National Data, https://
apps.bea.gov/iTable/iTable.cfm?reqid=19&step=2#reqid=19&step=2&isuri=1&1921=survey.

energy with higher-cost energy necessarily must reduce the aggregate supply of energy and thus energy use—an effect certain to reduce economic growth.

What follows is a discussion of several correlations of interest, but it must be kept in mind that correlation is not causation; correlations between given parameters can be spurious. The argument presented here is that these correlations are not spurious, but instead reflect important economic relationships. However, the magnitudes of the correlations must be interpreted with care because the correlations do not control for important influences not considered in the correlation computations.

Consider first the historical relationship between annual percent changes in energy consumption and economic growth, as illustrated in Figure 1.[18] The correlation between the two is 0.71 for 1980–2017, suggesting that energy consumption is an important parameter driving aggregate output and vice versa. These data suggest that one central

Figure 2. Energy Intensity of GDP

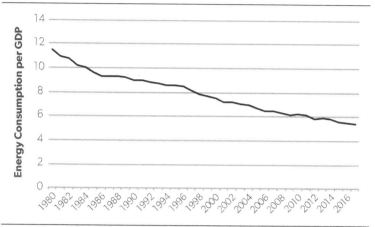

Source: US Energy Information Administration, Total Energy, https://www.eia.gov/totalenergy/data/browser/
index.php?tbl=T01.01#/?f=M; US Bureau of Economic Analysis, "Gross Domestic Product," https://www.
bea.gov/data/gdp/gross-domestic-product; and US Bureau of Economic Analysis, National Data, https://
apps.bea.gov/iTable/iTable.cfm?reqid=19&step=2#reqid=19&step=2&isuri=1&1921=survey.

premise underlying the GND proposals—less energy consumption caused by higher energy costs can yield stronger economic growth—is deeply problematic.

Figure 2 presents the 1980–2017 trend in the energy intensity of US GDP—that is, energy consumption per unit of economic output.[19] Since 1980, the amount of energy that the US economy uses to produce each dollar of GDP has declined by more than half, from about 11,500 British thermal units (Btu) per dollar of GDP to about 5,400. This trend is due primarily to increasing energy efficiency—technological advances—and to changes in the composition of US economic output.[20] But the ratio remains far greater than zero. These data suggest that a reduction in energy costs (or an increase in energy use) would encourage more economic output and that an artificial increase in energy costs would have the opposite effect.

Figure 3 presents the data on percent changes in energy consumption and employment for 1980–2017.[21] The simple correlation between the two series is 0.59. As in the case of GDP and energy consumption,

Figure 3. Annual Percent Changes: Employment and Primary Energy Consumption

Source: Federal Reserve Bank of St. Louis, FRED, s.v. "All Employees: Total Nonfarm Payrolls," https://fred. stlouisfed.org/series/PAYEMS; and US Energy Information Administration, Total Energy, https://www.eia.gov/ totalenergy/data/browser/index.php?tbl=T01.01#/?f=M.

it is clear from these data that employment and energy use are strong complements, suggesting that a reduction in energy costs (or an increase in energy use) would encourage more employment.[22] The opposite would be true for an increase in energy costs attendant upon the kind of artificial supply constraints envisioned in the GND.

The data presented in Figure 4 reinforce this inference on the ratio of employment to energy consumption—that is, the amount of employment "supported" by each unit of energy consumption.[23] Since 1980, that ratio has increased from about 1.2 to about 1.5. Despite—or perhaps because—the energy intensity of US GDP has declined, each unit of energy use has become more important in terms of its complementarity with employment. Accordingly, again, an increase in energy costs engendered by a policy-driven supply reduction would reduce employment; this issue is discussed further in Chapter 7.

Figure 4. Employment Intensity of Energy Consumption

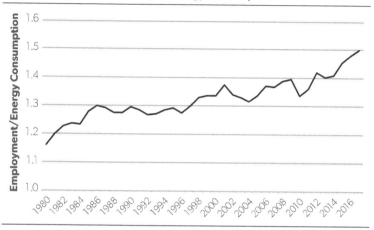

Source: Federal Reserve Bank of St. Louis, FRED, s.v. "All Employees: Total Nonfarm Payrolls," https://fred. stlouisfed.org/series/PAYEMS; and US Energy Information Administration, Total Energy, https://www.eia.gov/ totalenergy/data/browser/index.php?tbl=T01.01#/?f=M.

Figure 5 presents data on average household expenditures on utilities, fuels, and public services for all US households and for households in each income quintile, for 1984–2017, as reported by the Bureau of Labor Statistics (BLS) in its Consumer Expenditure Survey.[24] The inclusion of public services in this household expenditure series makes the data somewhat less than perfect for our purposes here, but it is obvious that these data are a useful instrument (or proxy) for the energy consumption parameter of interest, as this BLS series would be correlated closely with the energy expenditure data alone. Figure 5 illustrates the strong positive relationship between household income and expenditures on energy; each higher income quintile spends more on energy than the previous ones do. Since energy prices are unlikely to vary greatly across income classes—although the consumption mix of energy goods is likely to do so—energy is a "normal" good in economic language. Accordingly, factors that increase real incomes— investments in education, training, and health care are obvious examples—are almost certain to increase the demand for energy, an observation to which I return later.

Figure 5. Household Expenditures for Utilities, Fuels, and Public Services

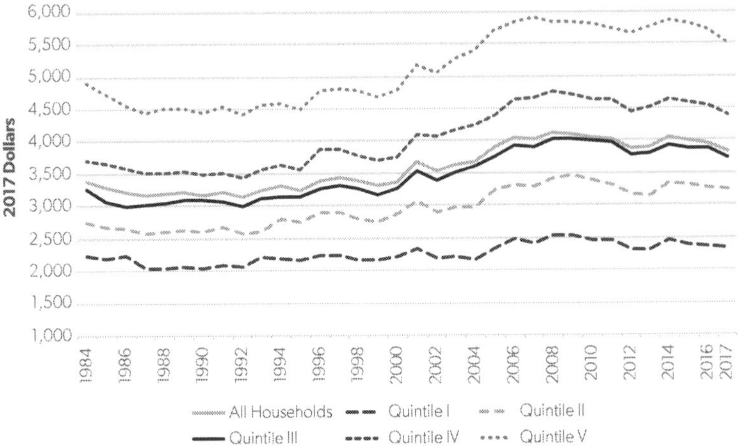

Source: US Bureau of Labor Statistics, Consumer Expenditure Survey, https://beta.bls.gov/dataQuery/find?st=18000&r=100&s=title%3AA&fq=survey:[cx]&more=0 and https://www.bls.gov/cex/; and Federal Reserve Bank of St. Louis, FRED, s.v. "Personal consumption expenditures (implicit price deflator)," https://fred.stlouisfed.org/series/DPCERD3A086NBEA.

We can use the annual BLS data on household incomes and spending on energy to compute the relevant correlations for each income quintile individually for 1984–2017; these computations are presented in Table 1.

The correlation is strong even for households in the lowest income quintile, and it increases sharply as we move to Quintile II and above. This striking fact is consistent with increasing energy demands as incomes rise, and it is consistent with the hypothesis that increasing energy use facilitates upward mobility for US households.

From Figure 5 (the increasing effect of household incomes on energy expenditures across income quintiles) and Table 1 (the high and rising correlations between household incomes and energy expenditures), it is reasonable to conclude that higher incomes induce households to consume more energy and perhaps that greater energy consumption is a factor yielding higher incomes.

Table 1. Correlations Between Household Incomes and Energy Expenditures, 1984–2017

Income Quintile	Correlation
I	0.55
II	0.89
III	0.92
IV	0.93
V	0.92
All	0.92

Source: Author computations based on US Bureau of Labor Statistics series on household spending on utilities, fuels, public services, and household before-tax incomes. US Bureau of Labor Statistics, Consumer Expenditure Survey, https://www.bls.gov/cex/; and US Bureau of Labor Statistics, "BLS Data Finder 1.1," https://beta.bls.gov/dataQuery/find?st=18000&r=100&s=title%3AA&fq=survey:[cx]&more=0.

This last point is worthy of some elaboration. If conventional energy is a social "bad" as assumed by GND proponents, particularly in a climate context, then by implication factors that increase individual and aggregate demands for conventional energy are social "bads" as well. In an aggregate sense, increasing GDP and rising employment are inconsistent with a reduction in the consumption of conventional energy and thus with the policy goals of the GND. At a household (or individual) level, rising incomes have the effect of increasing energy consumption, and the factors that improve incomes are similarly inconsistent with the policy goals of the GND. Those factors include greater employment opportunity, rising compensation for employed individuals, education and training investment, investment in productivity-enhancing capital, health care investment, and on and on. Do the proponents of the GND actually believe that they can change these fundamental relationships?

That such wealth-enhancing parameters fly in the face of the GND's objectives makes one central reality obvious: The GND at a fundamental level is antihuman in that its goals are diametrically opposed to the aspirations of nearly all individuals. GND proponents might respond that their objectives, whether climate related or otherwise, are more important than an advance in human

Figure 6. Energy Consumption and the Poverty Rate

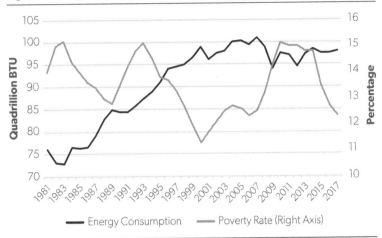

— Energy Consumption   —— Poverty Rate (Right Axis)

Source: US Energy Information Administration, Total Energy, https://www.eia.gov/totalenergy/data/browser/
index.php?tbl=T01.01#/?f=M; US Bureau of the Census, "Income and Poverty in the United States: 2017,"
September 2018, https://www.census.gov/library/publications/2018/demo/p60-263.html; and US Bureau
of the Census, "Impact on Poverty of Alternative Resource Measure by Age: 1981 to 2017," September
2018, https://www2.census.gov/programs-surveys/demo/tables/p60/263/Impact_Poverty.xls.

flourishing, but they should be forced to defend that proposition
explicitly.[25]

We have seen that energy consumption helps drive economic
growth (and vice versa) and the expansion of employment. That suggests that increasing energy consumption would be associated with
decreases in the poverty rate; those two data series for the US are presented in Figure 6.[26]

The correlation between the two is −0.44 for 1981–2017, though
the correlation fell (in absolute value) to −0.32 for 1997–2017.[27] The
absolute value of that correlation is striking, particularly given that
poverty is the result of numerous factors, among them poor-quality
education, various policies that reduce employment opportunity for
low-skilled workers, childbearing out of wedlock, and many other
causes, only some of which are understood well. Figure 7 presents
the trends for annual percent changes in energy consumption and
the poverty rate.

Figure 7. Annual Percent Changes: Energy Consumption and Poverty Rate

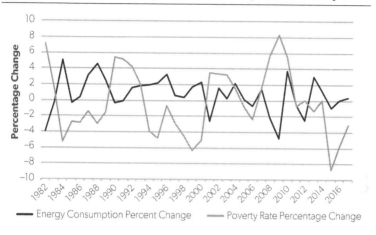

Energy Consumption Percent Change — Poverty Rate Percentage Change

---

Source: US Energy Information Administration, Total Energy, https://www.eia.gov/totalenergy/data/browser/index.php?tbl=T01.01#/?f=M; US Bureau of the Census, "Income and Poverty in the United States: 2017," September 2018, https://www.census.gov/library/publications/2018/demo/p60-263.html; and US Bureau of the Census, "Impact on Poverty of Alternative Resource Measure by Age: 1981 to 2017," September 2018, https://www2.census.gov/programs-surveys/demo/tables/p60/263/Impact_Poverty.xls.

For annual percent changes in energy consumption and the poverty rate, the simple correlation is −0.40, a figure surprisingly close to the correlation between the data trends (−0.44) shown in Figure 6. This correlation supports—but does not prove—the hypothesis that increasing energy consumption is a factor yielding a decline in the poverty rate, or that a reduction in energy consumption forced by such public policies as those proposed as part of the GND would tend to increase the poverty rate.

This last hypothesis is supported by the data summarized in Figure 8, showing the annual changes (first differences) in energy consumption and the poverty rate.[28] A high correlation between annual differences would be more powerful evidence of a causal relationship. That correlation for 1982–2017 is −0.38, which again supports the hypothesis that increased energy consumption is likely to reduce the poverty rate and that reduced poverty yields an increase in energy consumption.

Figure 8. Annual Differences: Energy Consumption and Poverty Rate

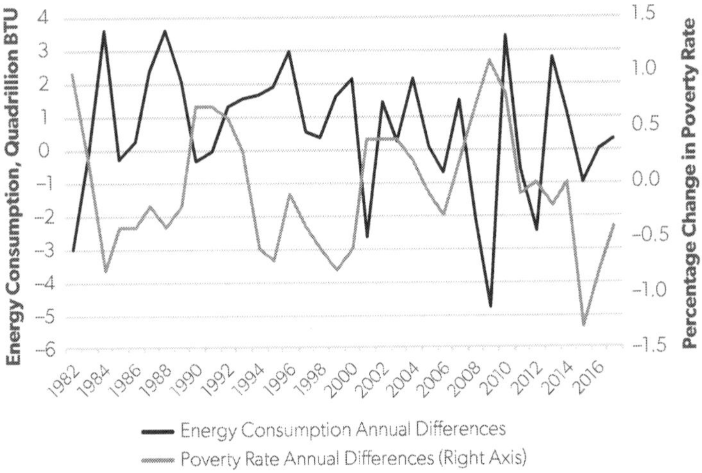

— Energy Consumption Annual Differences
⸺ Poverty Rate Annual Differences (Right Axis)

Source: US Energy Information Administration, Total Energy, https://www.eia.gov/totalenergy/data/browser/index.php?tbl=T01.01#/?f=M; US Bureau of the Census, "Income and Poverty in the United States: 2017," September 2018, https://www.census.gov/library/publications/2018/demo/p60-263.html; and US Bureau of the Census, "Impact on Poverty of Alternative Resource Measure by Age: 1981 to 2017," September 2018, https://www2.census.gov/programs-surveys/demo/tables/p60/263/Impact_Poverty.xls.

Figures 1–8 illustrate various relationships between energy consumption (or expenditures on such consumption) and other parameters. It is interesting as well to examine changes in primary energy production at the state level and the respective changes in household incomes and poverty rates and in unemployment rates.[29] For the US as a whole, primary energy production from 2000 to 2016 increased by 18.2 percent, while median household income (in constant dollars) from 2000 to 2017 increased by 2.4 percent.[30] The poverty rate declined from 12.4 percent in 2000 to 12.3 percent in 2017, while the respective figures for the unemployment rate were 4.0 percent and 4.4 percent, declining to 3.9 percent in December 2018.

For the lower 48 states (not including the District of Columbia), the simple correlation between the percent changes in primary energy production from 2000 to 2016 and median household income (2000 to 2017) was 0.17. These data are shown in Figure 9. Note that

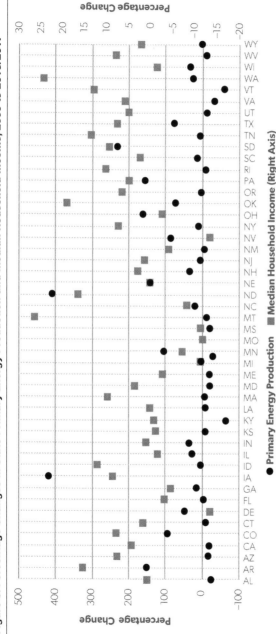

Figure 9. Percentage Changes in State Primary Energy Production and Median Household Income, 2000 to 2016/2017

Source: US Energy Information Administration, "State Energy Production Estimates 1960 Through 2016," 2018, https://www.eia.gov/state/seds/sep_prod/SEDS_Production_Report.pdf; US Census Bureau, "Table H-8. Median Household Income by State: 1984 to 2017," 2018, https://www2.census.gov/programs-surveys/cps/tables/time-series/historical-income-households/h08.xls; US Census Bureau, "Historical Poverty Tables: People and Families—1959 to 2017," August 28, 2018, Table 19, https://www.census.gov/data/tables/time-series/demo/income-poverty/historical-poverty-people.html; National Center for Education Statistics, Digest of Education Statistics: 2007, Table 20, https://nces.ed.gov/programs/digest/d07/tables/dt07_020.asp; Iowa State University, "Annual Unemployment Rates by State," https://www.icip.iastate.edu/tables/employment/unemployment-states; and US Bureau of Labor Statistics, Local Area Unemployment Statistics, https://www.bls.gov/lau/lastrk17.htm.

the data for primary energy production include energy production receiving large explicit and implicit subsidies; an example is ethanol production.[31] In principle, those subsidies should be excluded from the household income data, a complex calculation beyond the issues addressed here.

For the US as a whole, primary energy production from 2000 to 2016 increased by 18.2 percent, while the poverty rate from 2000 to 2017 declined slightly from 12.4 percent to 12.3 percent. Figure 10 shows the state-level percent changes in primary energy production for 2000 to 2016 and the percent changes in the state poverty levels for 2000 to 2017. The simple correlation between the two series is −0.09.

As the causes of poverty and changes in the poverty rate are complex, it would be surprising to find a high correlation between the two series illustrated in Figure 10. But the negative sign for that correlation is consistent with the general pattern of an expanded energy sector and reductions in poverty.

With respect to primary energy production and the unemployment rate for the US as a whole, the former increased by 18.2 percent from 2000 to 2016, while the unemployment rate increased from 4.0 percent in 2000 to 4.4 percent in 2017 (declining to 3.9 percent by December 2018). But for percent changes in the two series at the state level, the simple correlation is −0.03, a small number explained by the larger economic reality that an increase in employment in one sector (e.g., energy production) is likely to be offset by reduced employment in other sectors, other factors held constant.[32] Figure 11 displays the state trends for percent changes in primary energy production and in the unemployment rate.

The relationships shown in Figures 1–11 and in Table 1 suggest strongly that one central premise underlying the GND—that destroying the economic value of a substantial part of the US resource base and the energy-producing and energy-consuming capital stock would improve economic conditions and distributional equity—is diametrically opposed to reality. A reduction in energy consumption driven by public policies would harm economic growth. It is clear from the data that energy consumption and employment are strong complements, so a mandated reduction in energy consumption is likely to yield

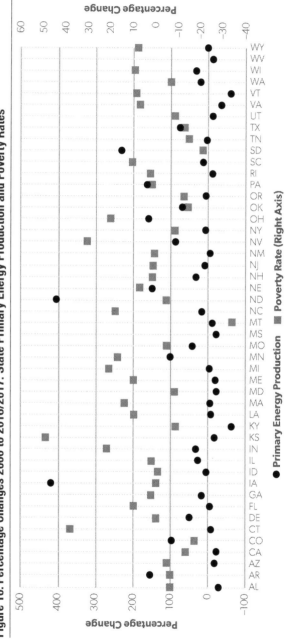

Figure 10. Percentage Changes 2000 to 2016/2017: State Primary Energy Production and Poverty Rates

Source: US Energy Information Administration, "State Energy Production Estimates 1960 Through 2016," 2018, https://www.eia.gov/state/seds/sep_prod/SEDS_Production_Report.pdf; US Census Bureau, "Table H-8. Median Household Income by State: 1984 to 2017," 2018, https://www2.census.gov/programs-surveys/cps/tables/time-series/historical-income-households/h08.xls; US Census Bureau, "Historical Poverty Tables: People and Families—1959 to 2017," August 28, 2018, Table 19, https://www.census.gov/data/tables/time-series/demo/income-poverty/historical-poverty-people.html; National Center for Education Statistics, Digest of Education Statistics: 2007, Table 20, https://nces.ed.gov/programs/digest/d07/tables/dt07_020.asp; Iowa State University, "Annual Unemployment Rates by State," https://www.icip.iastate.edu/tables/employment/unemployment-states; and US Bureau of Labor Statistics, Local Area Unemployment Statistics, https://www.bls.gov/lau/lastrk17.htm.

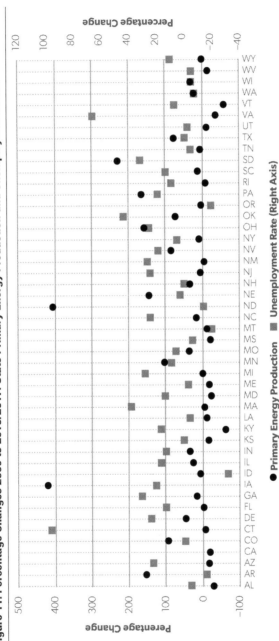

Figure 11. Percentage Changes 2000 to 2016/2017: State Primary Energy Production and Unemployment Rates

● Primary Energy Production ■ Unemployment Rate (Right Axis)

Source: US Energy Information Administration, "State Energy Production Estimates 1960 Through 2016," 2018, https://www.eia.gov/state/seds/sep_prod/SEDS_Production_Report.pdf; US Census Bureau, "Table H-8. Median Household Income by State: 1984 to 2017," 2018, https://www2.census.gov/programs-surveys/cps/tables/time-series/historical-income-households/h08.xls; US Census Bureau, "Historical Poverty Tables: People and Families—1959 to 2017," August 28, 2018, Table 19, https://www.census.gov/data/tables/time-series/demo/income-poverty/historical-poverty-people.html; National Center for Education Statistics, Digest of Education Statistics: 2007, Table 20, https://nces.ed.gov/programs/digest/d07/tables/dt07_020.asp; Iowa State University, "Annual Unemployment Rates by State," https://www.icip.iastate.edu/tables/employment/unemployment-states; and US Bureau of Labor Statistics, Local Area Unemployment Statistics, https://www.bls.gov/lau/lastrk17.htm.

adverse employment impacts. Because energy clearly is a normal good economically—higher incomes and wealth drive increases in energy consumption—an artificial increase in energy costs is inconsistent with the aspirations of those less fortunate for economic improvement. Moreover, it is obvious that policy-driven reductions in energy consumption are fundamentally antihuman, in that investments in human capital and other parameters that increase human well-being generally, and specifically the demand for energy, are inconsistent with the central policy objectives of the GND.

As noted above, correlation does not demonstrate causation. But increasing energy consumption is correlated with reductions in the poverty rate, and the data on annual differences in energy consumption and the poverty rate provide powerful evidence that this correlation is not spurious: An artificial reduction in energy consumption would tend to increase the poverty rate. Although the correlations are weaker with respect to energy production and the parameters of interest here, the state-level relationships between energy production and household incomes, poverty rates, and unemployment are consistent with the hypothesis that increased energy production is salutary with respect to those variables.

It is reasonable to ask that proposed public policies recognize these realities, in particular the central truth that the GND objective of substituting unconventional energy in place of conventional energy, or hindering the market development of energy resources, would be likely to worsen the lot of those with the lowest incomes. GND proponents seem to recognize that reallocating resources away from conventional energy sources and uses toward unconventional energy would create important economic losses during the transition—that is, during the economic "structural shift" engendered by the GND. The GND would require that investments be directed to

> spur economic development, deepen and diversify industry and business in local and regional economies, and build wealth and community ownership, while prioritizing high-quality job creation and economic, social, and environmental benefits in frontline and vulnerable communities, and deindustrialized communities, that

may otherwise struggle with the transition away from greenhouse gas intensive industries.[33]

Whatever the likelihood that a majority coalition enacting a GND would provide such transitional transfers to the specified beneficiaries, that "transition" passage by definition is a short-run orientation; it assumes away the long-run economic costs of the policy-driven reduction of energy supplies under the GND.[34] After the transition to a "clean" energy economy is complete, will the transfers remain a permanent feature of the policy landscape, as a response to the permanent reductions in real GDP and employment and increased poverty?

Note that the standard normative theory of government policy in the context of negative technological externalities[35] posits only that in a competitive sector in which prices do not capture such external impacts, market forces lead to an equilibrium in which excessive resource use is observed in that sector and too little in others.[36] This outcome requires the presence of transaction costs that prevent bargaining from internalizing the externality in the form of payment offers.[37] The normative prescription is that government adopt policies leading to a reduction in the output of the given sector (or a reduction in the use of inputs yielding the external effect); the public choice problem can be summarized as the issue of whether government under any given set of institutional arrangements has incentives (and the information) to adopt such policies.[38]

Nowhere does even that normative theory of government posit that entire sectors be shut down. That the GND proposals do precisely that implies a willingness to forgo all the economic benefits of that resource use; the discussion above summarizes some of them. Consider the Obama administration's Climate Action Plan, a large effort to reduce (not eliminate) US emissions of GHG through regulatory action.[39] The regulations were based analytically on a calculation of the "social cost of carbon" (SCC), conceptually the uninternalized adverse effects of US GHG emissions.[40]

That SCC calculation was replete with analytic errors and deeply problematic methodologies, the purpose of which was to increase the calculated SCC so as to justify a regulatory regime that the administration otherwise would not have been able to support under the public notice and comment requirements of the Administrative Procedures Act.[41] A good example is provided by the Obama administration's analysis of its proposed Clean Power Plan; the administration's own analysis showed net climate benefits close to zero.[42] Virtually all the asserted net benefits derived from air-quality co-benefits, that is, reductions in emissions of conventional pollutants already regulated under the Clean Air Act. Even that methodology was insufficient to yield an SCC calculation sufficiently large for the administration's political purposes, so the administration discounted the purported benefit stream at 3 percent, while it discounted the cost stream at 5 percent, thus increasing artificially the calculation of net benefits.[43]

The central point here is that the Obama administration did not contemplate a near shutdown of the conventional energy sector, and it is safe to assume that the large economic benefits of conventional energy are the central reason. In a recent working paper, Richard Tol reports[44] a calculation of the private economic benefits engendered by GHG emissions at $561–$611 per metric ton (in 2017 dollars) in 2014, figures vastly greater than the Obama administration calculation of the SCC at about $50 per ton.[45] US GHG emissions in 2016 were 6,511 million metric tons of CO_2;[46] Tol's calculation suggests an annual private economic benefit of US GHG emissions of about $3.7 trillion to $4.0 trillion.

In short, the economic benefits engendered by conventional energy use for individuals and for the economy in the aggregate are enormous, a reality shunted aside by GND proponents. Chapter 3 discusses the substantial environmental problems attendant upon an expansion of "clean" unconventional electricity generation and the implications of higher energy costs and reduced national wealth for aggregate political support for environmental protection.

3

Adverse Environmental Effects
of the Green New Deal

The GND will engender adverse environmental effects for a number
of reasons, including those discussed below.

"Clean" Electricity

With respect to the direct environmental effects of "clean" power generation, several serious adverse impacts not acknowledged by GND
supporters are of interest. In summary: There is the heavy-metal pollution created by the production process for wind turbines.[47] There
are the noise and flicker effects of wind turbines.[48] There are the large
problems of solar panel waste and toxic metals.[49] There is the wildlife
destruction caused by the production of renewable power.[50] There
also is the problem of massive land use, discussed below.

Economic Cost of Emissions from Backup Generation

It is technically impossible for a 100 percent renewable power system,
as defined in the GND, or anything approximating it to avoid both
frequent service interruptions ("blackouts") and a far smaller decline
than commonly assumed in emissions of conventional pollutants
and GHG. In other words, service interruptions are a crucial problem
under a 100 percent renewable power system, a problem that can be
addressed only with conventional backup capacity. This observation
requires a brief primer on the operation of an electric power system.

Electric energy in large amounts cannot be stored at low cost in
batteries due to technological limitations; only indirect storage in the

form of water in dams is economic. (The problems with battery storage are discussed in Chapter 4.) This reality means that the production and consumption of electricity in a given power network must be balanced constantly to prevent blackouts and more generally to preserve the expected reliability of the system.

Because unexpected surges in demand and/or outages of generating equipment can occur, backup generation capacity must be maintained; such backup capacity is termed the "operating reserve" for the given network. This operating reserve is of two types; the first is the "spinning reserve"—that is, generators already connected to the network, the output of which can be increased by raising the torque applied to the generating turbines. The typical system requirement is that spinning reserves be 50 percent or more of total operating reserves. The second component of operating reserves is the supplemental reserve, which comprises generation capacity that can be brought on line within five to 10 minutes and/or electric power that can be obtained quickly from other networks or by withholding power being distributed to other networks. Additional reserve capacity often is provided by generators that require up to an hour to come on line; this backup capacity is not included in measures of the operating reserve for a system because of the length of time required for availability.

Electric supply systems respond to growing demands ("load") over the course of a day (or year) by increasing output from the lowest-cost generating units first and then calling on successively more expensive units as electric loads grow toward the daily (or seasonal) peak. ("Baseload" units run more or less constantly except for scheduled and unscheduled downtime.) Electric generation capacity fueled by renewable energy sources is not "dispatchable"; that is, it is not available on demand because wind and sunlight are intermittent. In other words, system planning and optimization cannot be based on an assumption that it will be available to provide power to the grid when it is expected to be most economic. Accordingly, it cannot be scheduled: It requires backup generation capacity to preserve system reliability.

Several studies have concluded that wind capacity does not impose large reliability costs on a given power system as long as the wind generation remains about 10–20 percent or less of system output, because the intermittent nature of wind resources given a small market share has effects similar to those of unexpected outages and other familiar problems characterizing conventional generation.[51] At the same time, outages of wind capacity due to weak wind conditions are much more likely to be correlated geographically than is the case for outages of conventional plants, for the obvious reason that weak winds in part of a given region are likely to be observed in tandem with weak winds in other parts of that region. Because appropriate sites for utility-scale solar facilities (and rooftop photovoltaic systems) are concentrated geographically, the same correlation problem is likely to affect solar electric generation as well.

The problem of frequency regulation and grid stability—related to but distinct from the intermittency problem—created by a large expansion of non-dispatchable power generation is well-known.[52] In brief, most US generating capacity is alternating current (AC) and must be synchronized at 60 hertz. Because generation from wind and solar units cannot be ramped up and down in response to disequilibria in power frequencies in a grid, conventional units must be used to regulate those frequencies. Without such frequency regulation, the grid can become unstable, in the sense that the generators comprising the grid would be spinning at different speeds, a condition of nonsynchronous generation that can cause a power outage. In a critique of a proposal[53] for a 100 percent renewable power grid, Christopher Clack et al. make the following central observation.

An important gap in the analysis of [Jacobson et al.] is that it does not provide evidence that the proposed [100 percent renewable] system can maintain sufficient frequency regulation to preserve power system stability. The designers of power markets have known for decades that there is a need for improved markets that reward ancillary services that contribute to grid stability.

Further, [Jacobson et al.] state that [their] model "assumes a fully interconnected grid" that does not include any transmission constraints. [They] simply assume that there is unlimited transmission availability and that if "congestion is an issue at the baseline level of long-distance transmission, increasing the transmission capacity will relieve congestion with only a modest increase in cost."

This is a striking set of assumptions given that it has proven extremely difficult to site vital transmission lines, notably near urban areas (where loads are concentrated).[54]

In short, expansion of renewable power generation requires ancillary investment in backup capacity using conventional (dispatchable) technologies if frequent service interruptions are to be avoided. One major study of renewable systems worldwide finds that expanding dispatchable capacity by 1 percent facilitates an expansion of renewable capacity by 0.88 percent.[55] Tables 3 and 6 show that a GND renewable capacity investment requirement of about 2,627 gigawatts (GW) (wind and solar summed) would be a twentyfold increase over current wind and solar capacity of about 131 GW. If we assume, conservatively, that this renewable capacity investment would require dispatchable backup capacity of 15 percent, the latter would be about 394 GW.[56] It is reasonable also to assume a capacity factor of 40 percent for the backup units, as generation from wind and solar facilities is far more variable than that from conventional units, for which their backup units' capacity factors usually are assumed at 20 percent.

The direct costs of that dispatchable backup capacity and generation are discussed in Chapter 4. Of interest here are the economic costs of the emissions from that backup generation, as calculated in Table 2.[57] This estimate is based on the Obama administration calculation of the SCC, a deeply problematic analytic exercise.[58] Accordingly, the calculations in Table 2 are *not* an endorsement of the Obama SCC calculation or the proposition that CO_2 emissions impose important social costs; that is an issue outside the discussion here. (But the evidence on climate phenomena is discussed briefly in Chapter 7.)[59] Note that the Obama calculation of the SCC includes "co-benefits" in the form of reduced emissions of criteria pollutants—also a deeply problematic methodological approach—so that the CO_2 emissions entries in Table 2 are a straightforward proxy for all the emissions attendant upon the backup generation necessary under the GND electricity mandates.[60]

Table 2. Economic Costs of Natural Gas Backup Emissions

2017 Natural Gas Power Generation (tWh)	1,296.4
2017 Gas Combined Cycle Heat Rate (Btu/kWh)	7,649
2017 Natural Gas Consumption for Electricity Generation (Billion Cubic Feet)	9,250
2017 Natural Gas Consumption per tWh (Billion Cubic Feet)	7.1
2017 CO_2 Emissions from Natural Gas Power Generation (Million Metric Tons)	507
2017 CO_2 Emissions from All Power Generation (Million Metric Tons)	1,743
2017 Natural Gas CO_2 Emissions per tWh (Million Metric Tons)	0.4
2017 Natural Gas CO_2 Emissions per Billion Cubic Feet (Million Tons)	0.055
GND Annual Backup Generation per Year (tWh)	1,380.6
GND Backup Heat Rate (Btu/kWh)	8,424
GND Annual Backup Natural Gas Consumption (Billion Cubic Feet)	11,215.0
GND Assumed CO_2 Emissions per Billion Cubic Feet (Million Metric Tons)	0.055
GND CO_2 Emissions (Million Metric Tons)	616.8
Obama Administration Social Cost of Carbon (Dollars per Metric Ton)	$50.0
GND Annual Emissions Cost from Backup Generation (Billions of Dollars)	**$30.8**
GND Annual Emissions Cost per Backup mWh (Dollars)	$22.30
GND Annual Backup Emissions Cost per Household (Dollars)	$241.70

Source: Tables 3 and 5; US Energy Information Administration, *Electric Power Annual 2017*, December 2018, Table 8.2, https://www.eia.gov/electricity/annual/html/epa_08_02.html; US Energy Information Administration, "Natural Gas Consumption by End Use," February 28, 2019, https://www.eia.gov/dnav/ng/ng_cons_sum_dcu_nus_a.htm; US Energy Information Administration, *February 2019 Monthly Energy Review*, February 25, 2019, 209, Table 12.6, https://www.eia.gov/totalenergy/data/monthly/pdf/sec12_9.pdf; Interagency Working Group on Social Cost of Greenhouse Gases, "Technical Support Document: Technical Update of the Social Cost of Carbon for Regulatory Impact Analysis Under Executive Order 12866," August 2016, https://obamawhitehouse.archives.gov/sites/default/files/omb/inforeg/scc_tsd_final_clean_8_26_16.pdf; Gabriel Leon and Lourdes Mendoza Gonzalez, "Heat Rate Curve and Breakeven Point Model for Combine Cycle Gas Turbine Plants," ResearchGate, August 2018, Figure 10, https://www.researchgate.net/publication/327059862_Heat_rate_curve_and_breakeven_point_model_for_combine_cycle_gas_turbine_plants; and author's computations.

Moreover, unlike the GHG emissions goals of the Obama administration, the proponents of the GND argue for a virtual elimination of US GHG emissions. Implicitly, therefore, they must believe that the true SCC is vastly higher than that asserted by the Obama administration; certainly, they are in no position to argue that the Obama estimate is biased upward.[61] The Obama SCC of about $50 per metric ton of GHG emissions implies a cost for the GND backup emissions of $30.8 billion per year; the calculations are shown in

Table 2.[62] On a per-household basis, the annual cost would be about $242 per year.

Note from Table 2 that annual emissions from natural gas backup generation under the GND "100 percent renewables" mandate, perhaps surprisingly, would be 22 percent *higher* than the emissions from all 2017 natural gas–fired generation and over 35 percent of the emissions from *all* power generation in 2017. This is the direct result of the unreliability of renewable power: The backup units must be cycled up and down depending on wind and sunlight conditions, thus increasing heat rates (btu per kWh) and emissions.[63] The seriousness of this cycling problem is illustrated in Table 2: Annual natural gas backup generation under the GND would be over 6 percent higher than all natural gas generation in 2017, but emissions from natural gas backup power production, again, would be 22 percent higher. In short, the GND "100 percent renewables" mandate—even given the assumptions inherent in the GND policy proposals—to a significant degree is self-defeating as a purported solution to a climate crisis.

The Environmental Kuznets Curve

Chapter 4 expands the cost analysis to include the fixed costs of renewable power, transmission costs, the costs of backup power needed to avoid service interruptions, and the cost of land needed for the GND renewables mandate. As will be discussed, a conservative estimate of the annual cost of the GND electricity mandate alone is $490.5 billion. That cost would be about 2.5 percent of annual US GDP, which was about $19.5 trillion in 2018.[64] If we assume that long-run real GDP growth will average 3 percent annually, the annual economic cost of the GND renewable power mandate alone in effect would cut the annual real dollar increase in GDP by 83 percent.[65] Obviously, a smaller real GDP would increase the proportionate effects of the GND renewables costs, but I ignore here the direct effects of the GND's higher energy costs on GDP growth.[66]

This reduction in national wealth and household incomes in the US context can be predicted to reduce the individual, aggregate, and political willingness to pay for environmental protection generally, and for reductions in emissions of all pollutants in particular. This theoretical relationship—emissions rising and then falling as incomes rise—is known as the "environmental Kuznets curve."[67] The US clearly is on the portion of the curve displaying falling emissions as incomes rise. The goal here is not to construct an empirical estimate of the effect of reduced national wealth under the GND on environmental quality; that is a difficult topic fraught with complexities. But the potential effect should not be assumed away: The argument from GND proponents that a reduction in national wealth can be made consistent with increased environmental quality in the case of American democratic decision-making is deeply problematic.[68]

4

Direct Costs of the Green New Deal Renewable Electricity Mandate

The cost analysis presented in this chapter examines four dimensions of the GND renewable electricity mandate: the capacity and other fixed costs of wind and solar power, transmission costs for a greatly expanded renewable power system, the cost of backup power needed to avoid service interruptions under a "100 percent" renewable electricity mandate, and the cost of the land needed to site the new wind and solar facilities. The economic cost of the emissions resulting from backup generation needed to avoid blackouts was examined in Chapter 3.

Net Fixed Costs of Renewable Replacement Capacity

The cost of replacing the current electric generating system capacity mix with a new one comprising only "renewable" technologies is an exceptionally complex calculation that must be based on a set of reasonable but variable assumptions, in particular for the summary analysis presented here. Such a massive change in the capacity mix of the national electric grid would entail large additional costs for transmission and for investments in backup generating capacity needed to avoid service interruptions. Note that H.R. 109 calls for "meeting 100 percent of the power demand in the United States through clean, renewable, and zero-emission energy sources," suggesting that, in principle, fossil power generation might not be phased out completely if carbon capture and sequestration technologies, however costly, were adopted. Putting aside the immense costs of eliminating GHG emissions from fossil power generation, that language is inconsistent with the statement in the accompanying "Launch" document:

Table 3. US 2017 Net Summer Capacity by Energy Technology

Energy Technology	Generating Capacity (GW)
Coal	256.5
Petroleum	33.3
Natural Gas	456
Other Gases	2.4
Nuclear	99.6
Conventional Hydroelectric	79.8
Pumped Storage Hydroelectric	22.8
Wind	87.6
Solar Utility Scale	27
Solar Small Scale	16.1
Wood, Other Biomass, and Geothermal	16.4
Other	2.9
Total	**1,100.5**
Total Nonrenewable	**847.9**
Total Renewable	**252.6**
Total Nonrenewable/Total	**0.77**
Renewable/Total	**0.23**
Non-Hydroelectric Renewable/Total	**0.14**

Note: "Nonrenewable" includes coal, petroleum, natural gas, other gases, and nuclear. "Renewable" includes all others listed. Numbers may not sum due to rounding.

Source: US Energy Information Administration, *Electric Power Annual*, October 22, 2018, Table 4.3, https://www.eia.gov/electricity/annual/html/epa_04_03.html.

"We are calling for a full transition off fossil fuels and zero greenhouse gases."[69]

Table 3 presents the 2017 capacity mix of electric generation technologies for the US.[70] Total US generating capacity is about 1,100.5 GW, of which about 252.6 GW (23 percent) is renewable as defined in Table 3.[71] If we exclude hydroelectric capacity, renewable capacity is about 14 percent of the total.

Table 4 presents net electricity generation for 2017 by energy technology.[72] Total power generation in 2017 was about 4,046.7 terawatt-hours (tWh), of which renewable generation was about 17 percent, or about 10 percent if we exclude hydroelectric power from the definition

Table 4. US 2017 Net Electricity Generation by Energy Technology

Energy Technology	Electricity Generation (tWh)
Coal	1,205.8
Petroleum	21.4
Natural Gas	1,296.4
Other Gases	12.5
Nuclear	805
Conventional Hydroelectric	300.3
Pumped Storage Hydroelectric	−6.5
Wind	254.3
Solar Utility Scale	53.3
Solar Small Scale	24
Wood, Other Biomass, and Geothermal	67.1
Other	13.1
Total	**4,046.7**
Total Nonrenewable	**3,341.1**
Total Renewable	**705.7**
Total Nonrenewable/Total	**0.83**
Renewable/Total	**0.17**
Non-Hydroelectric Renewable/Total	**0.1**

Note: "Nonrenewable" includes coal, petroleum, natural gas, other gases, and nuclear. "Renewable" includes all others listed. Numbers may not sum due to rounding.
Source: US Energy Information Administration, *Electric Power Annual*, October 22, 2018, Tables 3.1.A and 3.1.B, https://www.eia.gov/electricity/annual/html/epa_04_03.html.

of "renewable." The respective capacity figures from Table 3, again, are 23 percent and 14 percent. So actual renewable electric output was about 4–6 percentage points lower than the respective figures for capacity, while nonrenewable sources were 77 percent of total capacity but 83 percent of actual generation.

The failure of non-hydroelectric renewable technologies to generate power in proportion to their capacities is driven by two factors. The first, mentioned here only in passing, is the theoretical limits constraining the production of electricity by wind and solar technologies.[73] The second, far more important in the context of the GND, is driven by the intermittent nature of wind flows and sunlight: Because the wind does not always blow and the sun does not always shine, and because neither is predictable when long-lived investment decisions are made or when system planning decisions must be made for day-ahead or even hourly markets, wind and solar power facilities have substantially lower "capacity factors" than is the case for conventional power technologies.[74]

This reality would be magnified under the GND mandate for two reasons. First, a geographic expansion of the renewables industry to many additional sites means that those sites inexorably will prove less and less suitable for renewable power production. After all, it is reasonable to assume that the first sites chosen were the best ones, controlling for political demands and other nontechnical influences that would not disappear under a GND, and that subsequent ones will exploit the next-best sites, with increasingly unsuitable ones used as the industry expands massively under a GND.

This process means that the renewable power sector will experience higher marginal and average costs for any given amount of power produced, particularly given that fixed costs are a far higher proportion of total costs for wind and solar power than for conventional generating technologies.[75] As the renewable industry expands substantially as a result of the policy-driven mandates of a GND, new facilities would be sited in areas increasingly unsuited for the production of wind and solar power, the upshot of which would be declining capacity factors both on the margin and on average for the industry as a whole.[76] Accordingly, the industry's declining capacity factors will be reflected in increasing scale diseconomies—rising average costs—as it expands sharply under a GND.[77] This is an important factor influencing transmission costs for wind and solar power, as discussed below. Moreover, the non-dispatchable nature of wind and solar capacity makes the capacity "credit" appropriate for a given renewable investment substantially lower than the "nameplate" (or official) capacity figure for that given unit. The Department of Energy provides analysis of this problem in the context of solar photovoltaic capacity.[78]

Second, wind facilities generate little power during summer peak-demand hours. For those summer peak periods, one estimate of the needed wind nameplate capacity to replace a given amount of

Table 5. Estimates of Capacity Factors for New Generation Facilities

| Technology | EIA | Capacity Factors (Percent) | | |
		Dept. of Energy	Lazard	IER
Conventional Coal (Without CCS)	85	N/A	93	54.6
Gas Combined Cycle	87	N/A	80	56.3
Nuclear	90	N/A	90	92.2
Wind (Onshore)	43	35	38	32.5
Solar (Photovoltaic)	33	N/A	34	28.6
Hydroelectric	65	N/A	N/A	35.9

Note: CCS is carbon capture and sequestration. IER estimates are not directly comparable to the others.

Source: US Energy Information Administration, "Levelized Cost and Levelized Avoided Cost of New Generation Resources in the Annual Energy Outlook 2018," March 2018, Table 1a, https://www.eia.gov/outlooks/aeo/pdf/electricity_generation.pdf; US Department of Energy, *2017 Wind Technologies Market Report,* August 2018, Figure 33; Lazard, "Lazard's Levelized Cost of Energy Analysis—Version 12.0," 2018, 13 and 15, https://www.lazard.com/media/450784/lazards-levelized-cost-of-energy-version-120-vfinal.pdf; and Thomas F. Stacy and George S. Taylor, "The Levelized Cost of Electricity from Existing Generation Resources," Institute for Energy Research, July 2016, 25, https://www.instituteforenergyresearch.org/wp-content/uploads/2016/07/IER_LCOE_2016-2.pdf. For coal capacity without carbon capture and sequestration (CCS), the EIA-assumed capacity factor is 85 percent. See US Energy Information Administration, *Annual Energy Outlook 2015,* Table A5, https://www.eia.gov/outlooks/aeo/pdf/appendix_tbls.pdf.

conventional fossil capacity is seven to nine times the fossil capacity to be replaced.[79] Accordingly, the needed amount of capacity for wind facilities replacing fossil generation during the summer is vastly understated here; this analysis assumes a factor of 2.9 to 1 (Table 6) rather than the more realistic 7–9 to 1.[80] Accordingly, the environmental damage caused by the GND replacement of conventional capacity with wind and solar capacity would be larger as well, and the ensuing need for proportionately greater backup generation by natural gas combined cycle plants would result in a proportionate increase in GHG emissions.

Table 5 presents four estimates of expected capacity factors for the power technologies of central interest here, from the Energy Information Administration (EIA), the Department of Energy (for wind), Lazard, and the Institute for Energy Research (IER).[81]

Note that the capacity factors shown in Table 5 are derived from observed operational parameters for the currently existing renewable power sector and for marginal increments. They do not envision a twentyfold increase in renewable capacity. Accordingly, for natural gas combined cycle, wind, and solar power, the respective capacity factors assumed here are 87 percent, 30 percent, and 25 percent. For wind and solar power, I assume capacity factors lower than the EIA estimates, in particular because of the scale diseconomy problem summarized above, a factor not incorporated in the various estimates presented in Table 5.

Let us now consider the magnitude of the conventional power generating capacity that would be replaced under GND policy of 100 percent "clean" and/or "renewable" electric generating capacity—that is, a replacement of plants using coal, petroleum, natural and other gases, and nuclear fuels. From Table 3, we see that the total 2017 capacity to be replaced would be 847.9 GW. Also from Table 3 we see that in 2017, wind capacity was 87.6 GW, while solar capacity (utility-scale and small-scale combined) was 43.1 GW. Accordingly, wind capacity was two-thirds of the total of the two, and solar capacity was the remaining one-third.

I assume here that the replacement of 847.9 GW of conventional power capacity with wind and solar capacity would be in that ratio. Moreover, in principle we should account for growth in US generating capacity as a response to increasing demand and other factors. But net summer capacity for the conventional plants listed above was essentially flat from 2007 through 2017; accordingly, we use 847.9 GW as the figure to be replaced in this GND conceptual experiment.[82] This assumption almost certainly biases the cost estimates downward, in that 2007–17 was a relatively slow period for GDP growth and thus for electricity demand conditions.[83]

Table 6 presents a computation of the wind and solar capacity investments needed to replace the 847.9 GW of conventional capacity. Because wind and solar facilities have capacity factors lower than those of the nonrenewable facilities to be replaced under a notional GND, the replacement cannot be assumed at a one-to-one ratio; instead, the differing capacity factors must be incorporated into a capacity factor adjustment so as to arrive at the amount of wind or solar capacity needed in theory to replace a given amount of

Table 6. Notional Wind and Solar Replacement Capacity Investment

Capacity Replaced (GW)	New Wind (GW)	New Solar (GW)	Wind Capacity Factor Adjustment (0.87/0.30)	Solar Capacity Factor Adjustment (0.87/0.25)	Adjusted New Wind (GW)	Adjusted New Solar (GW)
847.9	568.1	279.8	2.9	3.5	1647.5	979.3

Note: Assumes capacity factor of 87 percent for coal, gas, and nuclear facilities and 30 percent and 25 percent, respectively, for wind and solar facilities.
Source: Tables 3 and 5; and author computations.

nonrenewable capacity.[84] This approach still understates the amount of renewable replacement capacity needed to avoid outages, because unlike most maintenance and other such parameters, wind and sunlight conditions cannot be scheduled. These simple computations are shown in Table 6: Wind replacement must be 2.9 times the nonrenewable capacity to be replaced, while solar replacement must be about 3.5 times as much, in the 2:1 ratio already discussed.

Table 7 presents a calculation for the US as a whole of the annual cost of replacing all coal, gas, petroleum, and nuclear capacity with wind and solar facilities, in the 2:1 ratio discussed above.[85] As shown in Table 7, the annual net cost of the notional GND policy of 100 percent "renewable" power capacity replacement would be about $357 billion per year. As there are about 127.6 million households in the US (in 2018), the annual cost per household for wind and solar replacement capacity would be about $2,798.[86] The figures in Table 7 assume economic lives for the renewable capacity of 20 years; because that capacity would have to be replaced over time, the annual costs would be permanent.

Table 7. Net Annual Cost of Renewable Capacity Replacement for Nonrenewable Capacity (Billions of 2018 Dollars)

Component	Cost
Nonrenewable Capacity Replaced (GW)	847.9
Wind Replacement Capacity (Onshore) (GW)	1647.5
Wind Replacement Capital Cost	**2,675.5**
Wind Replacement Amortization Cost, Annual	211.9
Wind Replacement Fixed O&M Cost, Annual	79.8
Wind Total Replacement Cost, Annual	**291.7**
Solar Replacement Capacity (Tracking Photovoltaic) (GW)	979.3
Solar Replacement Capital Cost	**1,928.2**
Solar Replacement Amortization Cost, Annual	152.7
Solar Replacement Fixed O&M Cost, Annual	22
Solar Total Replacement Cost, Annual	**174.7**
Fossil Steam O&M and Fuel Savings, Annual	**−89.8**
Nuclear O&M and Fuel Savings, Annual	**−19.6**
Total Net Cost, Annual	**357**

Note: Costs are in billions of 2018 dollars. The wind adjustment factor is 2.9. The solar adjustment factor is 3.5. Annual amortization costs for wind and solar capacity assume 20-year asset lives and 5 percent interest rate.

Source: Tables 3, 5, and 6; US Energy Information Administration, *Electric Power Annual*, October 22, 2018, Table 4.3 and 8.4; and author computations.

Transmission Costs

Because wind and solar facilities must be sited where wind and sunlight conditions are most favorable, and because of low capacity factors, transmission lines must be longer and utilized less fully.[87] This is very different from the case for conventional power plants, which in principle can be sited almost anywhere, with fuels transported to the plants; system planning can optimize among site characteristics, transmission costs, and all the other factors affecting costs and technological parameters. Detailed estimates of generalized transmission costs for wind and utility-scale solar power are uncommon because they are highly idiosyncratic with respect to individual projects, but

Table 8. EIA Estimates of Levelized Transmission Costs (per mWh)

Generating Technology	Transmission Cost
Natural Gas Combined Cycle	1.0
Nuclear	0.9
Wind (Onshore)	2.4
Solar PV	3.3
Hydroelectric	1.8

Source: US Energy Information Administration, *Electric Power Annual*, October 22, 2018, Table 8.4; and author computations.

the EIA publishes each year in the *Annual Energy Outlook* a comparison of various components of the "levelized" costs of power produced with differing technologies.[88] With respect to transmission costs, the most recent EIA estimates are shown in Table 8.[89]

The transmission cost figure for natural gas generation is a reasonable proxy for all fossil electricity; transmission costs for wind and solar power are 2.4 times and 3.3 times higher, respectively. (I ignore here the small difference in transmission costs for nuclear power.) However, these EIA estimates are for the marginal costs of interconnection with the existing power grid given the current network of wind and solar facilities. They understate sharply the marginal costs of a transmission system incorporating, again, a twentyfold increase in wind and solar system capacity.[90] It is difficult to find in the literature an estimate of the additional transmission costs attendant upon so large an expansion of the renewable power sector, but clearly, the EIA estimates are biased downward substantially. For our rough purposes here, I assume a doubling of the cost figures per mWh for wind and solar transmission shown in Table 8: $4.80 for wind and $6.60 for solar.

From Table 4, the annual nonrenewable power generation to be replaced, using the 2017 data, would be 3,341.1 tWh. Under the same assumption as above that the replacement generation would be two-thirds wind and one-third solar, the additional annual transmission costs imposed by the electricity mandates of the GND would be $18 billion.[91] On a per-household basis, that is $141 annually.

Table 9. Cost of Backup Capacity and Generation for the GND Renewables System (Billions of 2018 Dollars)

Component	Cost
Backup Capacity (GW)	394
Backup Generation per Year (GW)	1380.6
Capacity Cost	$353
Capacity Cost, Annual Amortized	$28
O&M, Fuel Cost per Year	$48.9
Annual Cost	**$76.9**
Annual Cost per Backup mWh	**$55.7**
Annual Cost/Household	**$602.7**

Note: Costs are in 2018 dollars.
Source: Author's computations based on US Energy Information Administration, Total Energy, https://www.eia.gov/totalenergy/data/browser/index.php?tbl=T01.01#/?f=M; and US Energy Information Administration, *Electric Power Annual*, October 22, 2018, Table 8.4.

Cost of Backup Power

Table 9 constructs a cost estimate for the 394 GW of natural gas combined cycle backup capacity and annual backup generation of 1,380.6 tWh for the massive expansion of wind and solar capacity under the GND.[92] Backup costs on an annual basis would be $76.9 billion, or about $603 per household.

One alternative to the use of backup generation to stabilize the electric grid under a 100 percent renewables mandate would be simply to accept regular blackouts and their economic costs.[93] This alternative will not be explored here; the assumption is that the American body politic will not accept an electric power system characterized by a substantial degree of unreliability.

Another alternative, promoted by GND supporters, is the use of battery storage as a balance mechanism for an electric grid almost entirely comprising non-dispatchable generating units, a topic to which I turn briefly. Steve Huntoon discusses the massive problems with battery storage as an adjunct for renewable power; his central points, greatly simplified, are as follows.[94]

• Under assumptions highly favorable to the battery option, the latter is likely to be at least twice as expensive on an annual basis than the highest recent capacity prices observed in the PJM Interconnection.[95]

• Even that comparison is biased in favor of battery capacity because the economic lives of conventional generation units are substantially longer than those of the battery storage units. The discussion of the costs of renewable capacity (Table 7) assumes 20-year lives for the wind and solar capacity; Huntoon argues that is twice the economic life of the battery backup units in light of the limited evidence available.

• Batteries "generally can't sustain output for more than several hours," so battery backup is not wholly dispatchable.

Cost of Land

As discussed previously, the energy content of wind flows and sunlight is un-concentrated and depends on air speed and sunlight intensity, in contrast with the concentrated energy in fossil and nuclear fuels.[96] To compensate for the un-concentrated nature of renewable energy sources, large capital investments in land and/or materials must be made to make renewable generation even technically feasible in terms of generating nontrivial amounts of electricity. A wind farm would require 500 windmills of 2 MW each to provide a theoretical generation capacity of 1,000 MW.[97] Since the wind turbines must be spaced apart to avoid serious wake effects,[98] a theoretical 1,000 MW wind farm would require approximately 64,000 acres (100 square miles) of land. With an assumed capacity factor of 30 percent for a typical wind farm, actual wind capacity of 1,000 MW would require an area (perhaps at different locations) about three times that rough estimate.[99] In contrast, a 1,000 MW gas-fired plant requires about 30 acres; the analogous figures for coal and nuclear plants are 225 acres and 830 acres, respectively.[100]

The same problem characterizes solar power. The energy content of sunlight at the earth's surface is roughly 150–500 watts per square meter (W/m2), depending on location, of which about 20–30 percent is convertible to electricity, depending on the particular technology.[101] Accordingly, even in theory a square meter of solar energy receiving capacity is barely enough to power roughly one 100-watt light bulb, putting aside such capacity-factor issues of sunlight intensity and the like. This problem of land requirements for utility-scale solar facilities is sufficiently important that most analyses assume a maximum capacity of 50–100 MW, which, conservatively, would require approximately 1,250 acres, or about two square miles. The large Ivanpah solar facility in the California Mojave Desert has a gross capacity of 392 MW and sits on 3,471 acres, or about 5.4 square miles.[102]

From Table 6, the renewable replacement capacity required under the GND would be 1,647.5 GW for wind and 979.3 GW for solar. As a rough approximation, let us assume, conservatively, 64,000 acres (100 square miles) per 1,000 MW (1 GW) for wind capacity and 10,000 acres (about 15.6 square miles) per 1,000 MW for utility-scale solar capacity.[103] Under these rough but conservative assumptions, the land requirement for the new renewable generating capacity under the GND would be about 115.2 million acres, or about 180,000 square miles; that is over 15 percent greater than the land area of California.[104] This does not include transmission lines or other attendant infrastructure.

As land is not free, the cost of that land use is of central interest here. The US Department of Agriculture reports land values for farm real estate, cropland, and pasture acreage.[105] For the US as a whole, the lowest values among those three data series were for pasture acreage, at $1,350 per acre in 2017. For 115.2 million acres, that total land value is $155.5 billion; since land does not depreciate, the annual land cost is the perpetuity that has a present value of $155.5 billion at, say, a 5 percent interest rate. That annual figure for the cost of land needed for the GND renewables mandate is $7.8 billion, or $61 per household.

Table 10 summarizes the GND emissions and direct cost figures from Chapters 3 and 4. The average US retail price for electricity in 2017 was $104.80 per mWh; from Table 10, we see that a conservative estimate of the cost of GND renewable replacement power

Table 10. Emissions and Direct Costs of the GND Renewable Electricity Mandate

Category	Annual Cost (Billions of Dollars)	Annual Cost per Household (Dollars)
Emissions	30.8	242
Renewable Capacity	357.0	2,798
Transmission	18.0	141
Backup Power	76.9	603
Land	7.8	61
Annual Total	**490.5**	**3,845**
Annual Total per New Renewable mWh*	147.0	N/A

Note: *Assumes annual renewable replacement generation of 3,341.1 tWh. See Table 4. All dollar amounts are in 2018 dollars.
Source: Tables 2, 7, and 9; and author's computations.

would be $147 per mWh, or about 40 percent more than the average 2017 price.[106]

Average household incomes before taxes in 2017 were $73,573, $11,394, $29,821, $52,431, $86,363, and $188,103, for all households and for Quintiles I, II, III, IV, and V, respectively. From Table 10, a conservative estimate of the economic costs of the GND renewables mandate would be $3,845 per household, or 5.2 percent of average before-tax household income. That figure obviously would be higher if the cost were applied to after-tax incomes.[107]

Note also that these figures are the costs for only the electricity portion of the GND proposal. They do not include the massive costs of the shift away from fossil-fuel transportation or those of the proposed large-scale "high-speed rail," the "efficiency" retrofit of every building in the country, or the other social proposals in the GND. They also exclude adjustments for future economic growth and the resulting increase in the demand for energy, a reality that would increase the energy costs mandated by the GND.

The higher cost of electricity generated with renewable energy sources is only one side of the competitiveness question; the other is the value of that generation, as not all electricity is created equal. In particular, power produced at periods of peak demand is more valuable than off-peak generation, whether during a given daily cycle or across annual seasons. In this context, wind generation in particular is problematic because in general there are inverse relationships between the daily hours of peak demand and wind velocities and between peak summertime demands and peak wintertime wind velocities: Winds tend to blow at night and in the winter.

Paul Joskow notes that standard comparisons of levelized costs generally overvalue intermittent generating technologies such as wind power relative to dispatchable conventional generation.[108] Generating units that cannot supply reliable power when it is most valuable have lower economic value than alternatives that can, but our system of subsidizing renewable sources of electricity is based on the opposite assumption.[109] This problem is important for wind generation in particular because the output of wind facilities is disproportionately off peak, while solar generation tends to have the opposite characteristic: It is strongest during periods of peak daytime demand and during the summer. Levelized cost calculations do not incorporate this important factor.

The cost estimates presented above exclude large hidden costs worthy of some discussion, to which I now turn.

5

Large Hidden Costs of
the Green New Deal

Notwithstanding the lengthy list of social objectives of the GND, summarized in Chapter 1, the basic policy objective of the GND as asserted by its proponents is a reversal of an asserted climate crisis engendered by global GHG emissions. To the extent that the externality effects of increasing atmospheric concentrations of GHG are assumed to be negative globally, an attempt to reduce them is a classic collective (or public) good: The effects of such policies would be enjoyed or inflicted upon all, although the values placed on those effects certainly would differ, and those not contributing to the policy effort could not be excluded from the policy impacts.[110]

A number of observers have characterized the social objectives of the GND as a long step toward socialism or other similar summary descriptions.[111] But that orientation is not useful in thinking about the economic costs of the GND. Standard economic theory predicts that market competition will yield an allocational equilibrium in which collective goods are underprovided relative to the provision level that equates marginal social benefits and costs.[112] This yields the long-standing normative justification for government provision of collective goods, in which the implicit assumption is that government officials have incentives to discover and provide those efficient quantities. The difficulties inherent in that assumption are legion and well-known in the public choice literature; for our purposes here it is useful to examine how political incentives are likely to shape the responses of coalitions under democratic institutions.

Cost of Forging a Coalition for Provision of a Collective Good

Consider a world in which individual preferences for a collective good are known and can be aggregated (summed) across all voters and in which the marginal cost function is known as well. Therefore, the efficient quantity of the collective good (Q^*) also is known. In a simple model of majority decision-making, in which the median voter is the marginal member of the majority, assume that the government produces two goods: the collective good Q (say, defense) and a pure private good P (say, transfer payments).[113] Assume also that each unit of the two goods is a real dollar's worth, so that the price ratio between the two is 1:1. (In economic jargon, the slope of the budget constraint is –1.) Assume also that in a large political community ("polity") the majority is 50 percent of the electorate plus one voter. At Q^*, which lies on the budget constraint, the aggregated preferences also have a slope (the "marginal rate of substitution") of –1.[114]

But by virtue of the majority decision rule, the median voter decides the composition of the government output (or spending) basket of Q and P (defense and transfers).[115] In this simple model, the median voter—the majority—reduces spending on the defense good by $1 per voter and spends those resources on transfers of $2 per member of the majority. (The majority is almost exactly half the number of voters.) For the majority, every dollar per voter of reduced defense spending yields $2 per member of the majority. The majority in effect faces a budget constraint with a slope of –2 and chooses a budget shift such that the slope of the majority's preferences given the new basket of defense and transfers also is –2.[116]

In other words, voters and government too have powerful incentives to produce too few collective goods, and one way to reach a budget equilibrium in which provision of the collective good is at the efficient level is to offer more "pork"—wealth transfers—to forge a notional majority coalition. Put aside the "socialism" characterizations of the GND social agenda: The explicit effort through that social agenda to attract political support for the GND from numerous interests is the deeper meaning of those proposals, particularly in the context of an attempt to estimate the economic costs of the GND. Any such computation is beyond the scope of the analysis presented here, but some estimates available in the literature are:[117]

- $3.2 trillion annually for a single-payer health care system,

- $680 billion annually for an employment guarantee,

- $107 billion annually for "free college" and family and medical leave, and

- $200 billion annually for the high-speed rail component.

The sum is about $4 trillion per year, a number an order of magnitude greater than the (conservative) annual $490.5 billion cost of the renewable electricity mandate.

Marginal Excess Burden of the Tax System

However the GND costs are estimated, they represent real resources that government must marshal—that is, acquire from the private sector directly or indirectly—unless the renewable power costs are simply added to electricity bills, a topic addressed later in this chapter.[118] For the most part, acquisition of those resources is achieved through the tax system, whether during the current time period or some future one, and those who bear the economic burdens of such taxes can be predicted to attempt, *ceteris paribus*, to avoid them in whole or in part. Accordingly, particularly in the long run, taxes distort economic behavior, including work effort, saving and investment, transactions, and the like. Such distortions have the effect of lowering aggregate output below levels that would prevail without the taxes; that reduction in aggregate output, however hidden, is termed the "excess burden" of taxation.[119] In other words, taxes create an excess burden because the private sector bears a cost greater than a dollar to send a dollar to the federal government.[120]

This adverse economic effect of various federal tax instruments has been recognized broadly for many years, although there is a range of estimates on the size of the effects. There exists a substantial literature on the magnitude of the economic distortions engendered by the federal tax system; a somewhat older estimate is provided by Martin Feldstein.[121] Feldstein's finding, in brief, is that higher marginal tax rates used to finance additional federal spending would impose an excess burden of $0.76 per dollar of revenue; that is, it costs the private sector $1.76 ($1.00 of tax payments plus $0.76 of economic losses) to send an additional dollar to the federal government, other things held constant.

A recent survey of the literature finds a range of estimates, but a crude summary range is a marginal excess burden per revenue dollar of $1–$2, roughly double the Feldstein estimate.[122] Note that the marginal excess burden would rise as taxes rise and induce ever-greater distortions in resource use. If we assume a figure of $1.00 as the marginal excess burden of the tax system, the annual budget cost (excluding the annual $30.8 billion economic cost of backup emissions) of the electricity mandate financed federally would be about $460 billion plus another $460 billion (excess burden), or $920 billion. If we include the excess burden created by the annual $4 trillion cost of financing the unrelated programs needed to forge a GND political coalition, that total economic cost would be $8 trillion annually. It would be a vast understatement to say that the excess burden attendant upon financing the GND social agenda would be enormous.

Money Creation as a Financing Instrument

Some GND proponents have attempted to circumvent this obvious fiscal problem by arguing that the massive government borrowing required to finance the GND can be repaid through money creation. (A variant might be that no actual borrowing would be necessary: The Federal Reserve could simply create money through a keystroke, literally, to pay the GND bills.) The government can always print dollars to repay its (dollar) debts, a policy stance commonly referred to as Modern Monetary Theory, although government use of the printing press to acquire resources is old and familiar. Modern Monetary Theory is little more than the latest example of the old argument that there is available a free lunch, as illustrated by the argument from a prominent proponent that "anything that is technically feasible is financially affordable."[123]

Some critics of this argument note that it is correct narrowly—yes, government can repay its nominal debts if it creates the currency in which the debt is denominated—but that it would represent poor policy for various reasons.[124] The critics clearly are correct that government debt denominated in dollars can be "repaid" through money creation. But that observation is independent of the larger issue of whether the government borrowing needed to finance a GND would be possible in a world in which the market believes that the resulting debts will be repaid through money creation. Consider the dynamic effect of such government borrowing on the interest rate that it must offer.[125]

- A basic condition for the stability of government borrowing is that the real rate of return to government debt must exceed the growth rate of real government debt in the long run. If the market expects the debt to grow over the long term more quickly than the real return to the debt, then interest rates sufficient to induce the market to offer real resources to the government must increase, perhaps massively.

- The credibility of the government promise to repay its debts in real terms cannot be assumed to be independent of the magnitude of the debt itself, in that incentives to renege on promised debt service must rise as the debt rises. Moreover, potential lenders to the government would assume that dollar-denominated debts promising extremely high interest returns (say, 50 percent) in fact would not be repaid in real terms, as the incentive to renege would become overwhelming.

- If incentives for the government to use money creation to repay nominal debts are seen as strengthening significantly, interest rates would rise to reflect the risk of default in real terms, that is, repayment in dollars buying fewer real goods and services.

This last point brings us to the obvious inflation problem attendant upon Modern Monetary Theory. Unless massive money creation is assumed to lead to a decline in the income velocity of money—crudely, the rate at which dollars are spent—which is a deeply problematic assumption, then a sharp increase in the money supply must create an inflation, unless somehow there is an increase in the real resources available to the private sector.[126] But the GND assumes a massive resource shift toward the government, in this case through the mechanism of government borrowing.

Accordingly, a sharp increase in inflation is the inexorable implication of Modern Monetary Theory. To the extent that an inflation is anticipated, it is a tax on non-interest-bearing money, which is another way of seeing that a GND financed through borrowing to be repaid with money creation must increase velocity, as individuals attempt to avoid this tax by reducing their holdings of money. To the extent that the inflation is not anticipated, it is a subsidy for nominal debtors, financed by a tax on nominal creditors, who would receive debt repayment in nominal dollars that purchase less than anticipated in real goods and services. Notice that government is always a net monetary debtor, so the upshot of Modern Monetary Theory is a massive wealth transfer to the government—that is, to the interests benefiting from government borrowing.[127]

The proponents of Modern Monetary Theory as a financing mechanism for the GND respond that the inflation problem can be avoided by using taxes to remove money from the economy, thus easing the inflationary effect, a proposed transformation of fiscal policy into a substitute for monetary policy.[128] This is little more than saying that the GND borrowing would be financed through explicit taxation, with the large adverse excess burden effects discussed above. At a more general level, the proponents of GND finance with a system of debt "repayment" through money creation are arguing in a nutshell that the government will be able to borrow real resources from the private sector and then repay the debts without transferring real resources in return. No one can believe that markets are that myopic. There are no free debt lunches.

Consider a GND to be financed through a fully anticipated inflation, constituting a tax on non-interest-bearing money. Assume also that all money except currency earns interest. Currency in circulation is about $1.7 trillion.[129] If we assume, conservatively, that a GND financed with money creation would result in an anticipated inflation of 10 percent per year, then the implicit tax on currency, yielding a transfer of real resources to the government, would be about $170 billion per year. Note that this tax is less than the cost to the economy inflicted by the inflation, as individuals and businesses take actions to protect themselves from this tax. This is another dimension of the excess burden attendant upon governmental acquisition of real resources; estimates of this effect vary, but one survey of the literature finds:

> A number of empirical studies have sought to measure the interactions between inflation and the nominal nature of the U.S. tax system. Most find the costs are large. Authors James Bullard and Steven Russell, for example, suggest approximately a 1 percent output loss for each 1 percent increase in inflation above price stability.[130]

This inflationary version of the excess burden created by the government acquisition of resources would take the form of such adverse consequences as a degradation of the currency as a store of value, adverse behavioral responses by holders of currency, and the like. The use of money creation to service debt incurred to finance the GND also is deeply dubious, as any such approach would be based on an assumption that purchasers of government debt instruments will deliver real resources to the government with no expectation of receiving repayment in an equivalent amount of real resources, plus interest. It cannot be the case that lenders to the government are so myopic.

From the discussion above, a downward-biased estimate of the annual hidden costs of the GND can be summarized as follows in Table 11.

Table 11. Annual Hidden Costs of the GND (Billions of 2018 Dollars)

GND Policy	Cost
Budget Cost of Forging a GND Coalition	4,000
Excess Burden of Tax System	
Renewable Power Mandate	460
GND Coalition	4,000
Total	**8,460**

Source: Author's computations.

State-by-State Cost Analysis Under a Ratepayer Finance Assumption

The discussion in Chapters 4 and 5 assumes that the massive costs of the GND would be borne, at least formally, at the federal level rather than as increases in the electricity rates paid by ratepayers. That discussion suggests the difficulty of such a federal financing role for the GND, although federal financing through the tax system or debt or inflationary finance would tend to hide the costs to a substantial degree. An alternative would be to pay for the power system costs ($490.5 billion annually) at the state level through electricity rates, a financing approach that would hide those costs to a far smaller degree.

Because of substantial variation in the capacity mix of generation technologies across the states, the costs both in total and per household would vary also. Table 12 presents the annual cost components, annual total costs, and annual cost per household by state, following the aggregate calculations for the US as a whole as shown in Table 10. These state-by-state calculations are rough, in that they assume that the costs are proportional to the nonrenewable generating capacity to be replaced in each of the respective states. Accordingly, these cost numbers for the individual states are only first approximations and must be interpreted carefully because they do not account for exports and imports of power among the states (and from Canada). Given the central methodologies used for power system ratemaking at the state level, it is reasonable to assume that consumers using power imported from other states would pay most of the cost of replacing fossil and nuclear power with wind and solar power delivered across state lines under a ratepayer finance assumption for the GND. However, the simple correlation between changes (first differences) in individual state generation and sales from 2016 to 2017 is 0.38, suggesting that the estimates reported in Table 12 are useful as rough approximations.

Table 12. Lower 48 States: Annual Net Cost of GND Renewable Electricity Mandate Under Ratepayer Finance (Billions of 2018 Dollars)

State	Capacity Replacement	Transmission	Backup	Emissions	Land	Total	Households (Millions)	Per Household ($)
AL	10.8	0.5	2.3	0.9	0.2	14.8	1.8	8,049
AR	5.5	0.3	1.2	0.5	0.1	7.5	1.2	6,539
AZ	9.8	0.5	2.1	0.8	0.2	13.5	2.6	5,286
CA	17.9	0.9	3.8	1.5	0.4	24.5	13	1,885
CO	4.7	0.2	1	0.4	0.1	6.5	2.1	3,028
CT	3.5	0.2	0.7	0.3	0.1	4.7	1.4	3,488
DE	1.4	0.1	0.3	0.1	0	1.9	0.4	5,303
FL	23.9	1.2	5.2	2.1	0.5	32.9	7.7	4,273
GA	13.1	0.7	2.8	1.1	0.3	18	3.8	4,798
IA	4.4	0.2	1	0.4	0.1	6.1	1.3	4,821
ID	0.5	0	0.1	0	0	0.6	0.6	1,010
IL	17.1	0.9	3.7	1.5	0.4	23.5	4.8	4,883
IN	9.8	0.5	2.1	0.8	0.2	13.4	2.6	5,243
KS	4.6	0.2	1	0.4	0.1	6.4	1.1	5,631
KY	8	0.4	1.7	0.7	0.2	10.9	1.7	6,320
LA	9.6	0.5	2.1	0.8	0.2	13.1	1.7	7,547
MA	3.8	0.2	0.8	0.3	0.1	5.3	2.6	2,025
MD	5.1	0.3	1.1	0.4	0.1	6.9	2.2	3,141
ME	1.1	0.1	0.2	0.1	0	1.4	0.5	2,678
MI	10.5	0.5	2.3	0.9	0.2	14.4	3.9	3,665
MN	4.9	0.2	1.1	0.4	0.1	6.8	2.2	3,133
MO	8.3	0.4	1.8	0.7	0.2	11.3	2.4	4,764
MS	6.5	0.3	1.4	0.6	0.1	8.9	1.1	8,173
MT	1.1	0.1	0.2	0.1	0	1.6	0.4	3,719
NC	11.2	0.6	2.4	1	0.2	15.4	4	3,900
ND	1.9	0.1	0.4	0.2	0	2.7	0.3	8,316
NE	2.9	0.1	0.6	0.3	0.1	4	0.8	5,322
NH	1.5	0.1	0.3	0.1	0	2	0.5	3,820

(continued on the next page)

State	Capacity Replacement	Transmission	Backup	Emissions	Land	Total	Households (Millions)	Per Household ($)
NJ	6.9	0.4	1.5	0.6	0.2	9.5	3.2	2,964
NM	2.5	0.1	0.5	0.2	0.1	3.5	0.8	4,508
NV	3.3	0.2	0.7	0.3	0.1	4.5	1.1	4,140
NY	13.2	0.7	2.8	1.1	0.3	18.2	7.3	2,488
OH	12.2	0.6	2.6	1.1	0.3	16.8	4.7	3,592
OK	7.8	0.4	1.7	0.7	0.2	10.8	1.5	7,320
OR	1.8	0.1	0.4	0.2	0	2.5	1.6	1,555
PA	16.6	0.8	3.6	1.4	0.4	22.8	5	4,549
RI	0.8	0	0.2	0.1	0	1	0.4	2,540
SC	7.6	0.4	1.6	0.7	0.2	10.4	1.9	5,452
SD	0.7	0	0.2	0.1	0	1	0.3	2,892
TN	6.9	0.3	1.5	0.6	0.2	9.5	2.6	3,663
TX	41.4	2.1	8.9	3.6	0.9	56.9	9.6	5,911
UT	3.1	0.2	0.7	0.3	0.1	4.2	1	4,309
VA	9.4	0.5	2	0.8	0.2	12.9	3.1	4,135
VT	0	0	0	0	0	0.1	0.3	222
WA	2.5	0.1	0.5	0.2	0.1	3.5	2.8	1,222
WI	6.6	0.3	1.4	0.6	0.1	9.1	2.4	3,865
WV	5.8	0.3	1.3	0.5	0.1	8	0.7	11,088
WY	2.9	0.1	0.6	0.2	0.1	3.9	0.2	17,103
US	357	18	76.9	30.8	7.8	490.5	127.6	3,845

Note: Totals may not sum due to rounding.
Source: Author's computations.

The annual household costs range from $222 for Vermont to $17,103 for Wyoming. These calculations are rough and do not account for changes in employment and earnings that would result from a major increase in energy costs attendant upon the GND. But they are meaningful in that they are likely to be correlated closely with a broader measure incorporating those parameters, a complex calculation outside the scope of the analysis here.

It is interesting to recognize the obvious truism that politics is the art of wealth redistribution, and public officials constrained by the demands and pressures of electoral politics have powerful incentives to avoid proposed policies that transfer wealth away from their constituents or their marginal voters. Accordingly, it is worth noting that the simple correlation between the annual state-by-state household costs of the GND (again, under a ratepayer finance assumption) and the respective state vote percentages in 2016 for then-candidate Donald Trump is 0.71.

Note that the forced retirement of the conventional capacity mandated under the GND would relieve ratepayers of the costs of fuel and both fixed and variable operations and maintenance (O&M), as shown in Table 7. But the undepreciated remaining (historical) costs of the generation capacity itself would remain to be paid and thus would continue to be included in ratepayers' bills, unless, again, the costs were shifted under a GND to federal taxpayers or other groups, depending on how the government acquires the resources needed to finance the GND. An attempt to deny shareholders recovery of those costs almost certainly would be struck down by the courts as a taking of private property for public use without just compensation under the Fifth Amendment, particularly given that those historical capital costs would have been approved earlier as "prudent" or as "used and useful" by the respective state regulatory authorities.[131] Accordingly, the net costs per household would be added to ratepayers' bills, with the same caveat as above.

6

Inexorable Authoritarian Implications of the Green New Deal

Consider the recent drought conditions afflicting California, largely ameliorated by significant rainfall and snowfall thus far in the 2019–20 water year. NASA notes:

> The current drought is not part of a long-term change in California precipitation, which exhibits no appreciable trend since 1895. Key oceanic features that caused precipitation inhibiting atmospheric ridging off the West Coast during 2011–14 were symptomatic of natural internal atmosphere-ocean variability.[132]

In other words, drought conditions in California are nothing new and cannot be blamed on atmospheric concentrations of GHG. However, it is clear that various public policies are responsible for the adverse effects of recent low precipitation in the state, particularly water availability for agriculture, urban use, and the like.[133] Those policies and their effects are not of direct interest here. What is of interest is the recent response of the California state government to the then-perceived drought-related shortage of water. In brief: State law now limits indoor water use to 55 gallons per person per day in 2022, declining to 50 gallons in 2030.[134]

How would this be enforced? It is obvious that government, whether directly or indirectly through such intermediaries as water utilities, would use existing or new water meters to monitor water consumption. And the per-person consumption limits suggest that government also would find it necessary, or expedient, to monitor the number of individuals in a household. In other words, a water crisis engendered wholly or substantially by government has become a rationale for a sharp increase in the surveillance activities of government.

In the context of the GND, notice that it calls for a national "smart grid," defined by the US Department of Energy as a system of

> digital technology that allows for two-way communication between the utility and its customers, and . . . sensing along the transmission lines. . . . Like the Internet, the Smart Grid will consist of controls, computers, automation, and new technologies and equipment working together, but in this case, these technologies will work with the electrical grid to respond digitally to our quickly changing electric demand.[135]

How would such "two-way communication between the utility and its customers" be achieved? This would require the widespread installation of "smart meters," one standard definition of which is as follows.

> Smart meters, a common form of smart grid technology, are digital meters that replace the old analog meters used in homes to record electrical usage. *Digital meters can transmit energy consumption information back to the utility on a much more frequent schedule than analog meters*, which require a meter reader to transmit information.
>
> Electric energy use will be recorded every hour or less at your home. Smart meters will enable you to monitor your consumption more precisely so you can make more informed energy choices. Depending on the feature set, the meter may also notify the utility of a power outage *or allow the utility to remotely switch electricity service on or off.* [136] [Emphasis added.]

Since government regulates virtually all utilities, it is easy to envision a requirement that they report consumption data, or perhaps outlying consumption data, to regulatory and/or other authorities. Indeed, it is difficult to envision an absence of such a requirement. And whatever the utility's justifications for "remotely switch[ing] electricity service on or off," it is difficult to believe that government regulators systematically will refrain from ordering regulated utilities to do the same, for reasons serving political purposes.

Recall the discussion above of the inherent unreliability of wind and solar power; it is not dispatchable. If the proponents of the GND are serious about the policy goal of zero (or net zero) GHG emissions, then one unavoidable consequence in the absence of large amounts of conventional backup capacity would be regular service interruptions (blackouts), whether afflicting narrow or large geographic areas in any given instance. Just as in the case of water rationing in California, it is inevitable that some form of rationing for power supplies during outages would be implemented; it is literally the case that no other outcome is possible. To whom will valuable power supplies be allocated during periods of peak demand or supply outages? Is it even conceivable that political criteria will not be brought to bear on this question? Which industries and geographic regions will policymakers favor? And what demands will politicians and bureaucratic officials make, whether explicit or implicit, in return for keeping the lights on? To put it differently, the costs of blackouts will be very large indeed, matched by the political incentives to use those costs to transfer wealth to favored constituencies.

In other words, the central feature of the smart grid component of the GND will be a substantial increase in government surveillance of electricity use and the use of those data in the context of power shortages to reward friends and punish enemies. If this is not authoritarianism, what is?

With respect to the transportation sector, House of Representative Resolution 109 establishes as a goal an overhaul of

> transportation systems in the United States to remove pollution and greenhouse gas emissions from the transportation sector as much as is technologically feasible, including through investment in—(i) zero-emission vehicle infrastructure and manufacturing; (ii) clean, affordable, and accessible public transportation; and (iii) high-speed rail.[137]

Technological feasibility imposes virtually no upper constraint on the costs of this transformation and no lower constraint on the benefits. Accordingly, it implies an elimination of the internal combustion engine from the transportation sector, and it is not clear whether under the GND fossil-fuel backup generation would be allowable for recharging electric vehicles. Presumably the answer is no, given the requirement that US "transportation systems . . . remove pollution and greenhouse gas emissions from the transportation sector," and the same seems to be true for the vehicle and battery production systems, constrained by the requirement for "zero-emission vehicle infrastructure and manufacturing."

This policy would engender an enormous wealth transfer from rural, exurban, and suburban areas to urban ones, as individuals and businesses are forced by artificial transport constraints to concentrate in urban centers. Perhaps more important in the context of authoritarianism, this dimension of the GND would result in a sharp reduction in individual mobility. That is the direct implication of a policy designed explicitly to force a massive shift toward transportation modes characterized by sharply limited ranges, time-consuming recharging processes, and the severe constraints imposed by government rationing of electricity supplies under the frequent blackout conditions created by a "100 percent" renewable power mandate. Is it impossible to believe that siting of auto recharging stations outside urban areas would receive a low political priority or that the "smart meter" system would lead to government snooping on individuals surreptitiously recharging the vehicles at night?

Moreover, the requirement for a large expansion of "clean, affordable, and accessible public transportation and high-speed rail" means that to a significant degree government would decide where people can travel. Is it actually the position of the GND proponents that these routing decisions would not be politicized or that a sharply reduced individual ability to decide where to go and when would not represent a major loss of individual freedom?[138] Moreover, if the purported climate crisis truly is existential, then it is not clear what limiting principle applies to efforts to achieve zero GHG emissions, including tracking surveillance of automobile movements, perhaps through GPS technology. At a minimum, it is wholly plausible that owners of private vehicles would be required to install tracking devices or at least mileage metering equipment, the data to be reported to appropriate authorities one way or another. No great imagination is required to envision the authoritarian objectives for which such data inevitably would be used.

7

Observations on Some Ancillary Topics

The GND proposal raises several important related issues, observations about which are as follows.

Green Employment

A common argument in support of expanded renewable power posits that policies (subsidies) in support of that goal will yield important benefits in the form of complementary employment growth in renewables sectors and stronger demand in the labor market in the aggregate.[139] Both of those premises are almost certainly incorrect.

To begin, employment in renewables sectors created by renewables policies actually would be an economic cost rather than a benefit for the economy as a whole. Suppose that policy support for renewables (or for any other sector) were to increase the demand for, say, high-quality steel. That clearly would be a benefit for steel producers, or more broadly, for owners of inputs in steel production, including steel workers. But for the economy as a whole, the need for additional high-quality steel in an expanding renewable power sector would be an economic cost, as that steel (or the resources used to produce it) would not be available for use in other sectors, the very definition of an economic cost. Similarly, the creation of "green jobs" as a side effect of renewables policies is a benefit for the workers hired (or for those whose wages rise with increased market competition for their services). But for the economy as a whole, that use of scarce labor is a cost because those workers no longer would be available for productive activity elsewhere.[140]

More to the point, an expansion of the renewable electricity sector must mean a decline in some other sector(s), with an attendant reduction in resource use there; after all, resources in the aggregate are finite. If there exists substantial unemployment and if labor demand in renewables is not highly specialized, a short-run increase in total employment might result. But in the long run—not necessarily a long period of time—such industrial policies cannot "create" employment; they can only shift it among economic sectors. In short, an expanding renewables sector must be accompanied by declines in other sectors, whether relative or absolute, and creation of "green jobs" must be accompanied by a destruction of employment elsewhere. Even under the questionable assumption that an expanding renewables sector is more labor intensive (per unit of output) than the sectors that would decline as a result, it remains the case that the employment expansion would be a cost for the economy as a whole, and the aggregate result would be an economy smaller than otherwise would be the case, as labor resources would be reallocated to less-productive uses.[141]

There is no particular reason to believe that the employment gained as a result of the (hypothetically) greater labor intensiveness of renewables systematically would be greater than the employment lost because of the decline of other sectors, combined with the adverse employment effect of the smaller economy in the aggregate. There is also the adverse employment effect of the large explicit or implicit tax increase that must be imposed to finance the expansion of renewable power.

Note also from Figure 3 that energy consumption and employment are strong complements. As electricity costs and prices rise, and aggregate output falls, under a GND, it is almost axiomatic that employment will fall as well, in particular given that the cost of using equipment and other such capital complementary with labor employment would rise.[142]

It certainly is possible that the historical relationship between employment and energy consumption will change. Technological advances are certain to occur, but the prospective nature and effects of those shifts are difficult to predict.[143] The US economy may evolve over time in ways yielding important changes in the relative sizes of industries and sectors, as it has continually over time, but again, the direction of the attendant shifts in employment and electricity use is ambiguous.

But there exists no evidence with which to predict that a reduction in electricity consumption would yield an increase in employment. Like all geographic entities, the US has certain long-term characteristics—climate, available resources, geographic location, trading partners, legal institutions, ad infinitum—that determine in substantial part the long-run comparative advantages of the economy in economic activities and specialization.

Sustainability

"Renewable" energy has no uniform definition, in particular given the disagreements among proponents on the role of hydroelectric and nuclear power. But the (assumed) finite physical quantity of such conventional energy sources as petroleum is the essential characteristic differentiating the two in most discussions.[144] In a word, conventional energy sources physically are (assumed to be) depletable. In contrast, each sunrise and geographic temperature differential yields new supplies of sunlight and wind flows, a central component of "sustainability," which perhaps is a concept broader than the depletion condition. Nonetheless, the definition of "sustainability" is highly elusive, as this Environmental Protection Agency (EPA) discussion illustrates.

> Sustainability is based on a simple principle: Everything that we need for our survival and well-being depends, either directly or indirectly, on our natural environment. To pursue sustainability is to create and maintain the conditions under which humans and nature can exist in productive harmony to support present and future generations.[145]

This is blather, definitive proof that the EPA has no idea what "sustainability" means as an analytic concept. An international definition often cited is from the United Nations.

> Humanity has the ability to make development sustainable to ensure that it meets the needs of the present without compromising the ability of future generations to meet their own needs.[146]

This definition also is useless, as "needs" whether present or future are undefined, and the evaluation of the inexorable trade-offs among such needs is ignored. Whether in the present or the future or across time periods and generations, the effects of technological advances unknown but certain to occur are not considered, ad infinitum. The interests of future generations are discussed below.

In any event, the energy content of sunlight and wind is finite, regardless of whether new supplies of sunlight or wind flows emerge continually. They contain only so much convertible energy, which is not always available. Moreover, the same is true for the other resources—materials, land, etc.—on which the conversion of such renewable energy into electricity depends. More fundamentally, the basic "sustainability" concept seems to be that without policy intervention, the operation of market forces will result in the depletion (or exhaustion) of a finite resource. Accordingly, subsidies and other support for renewable power generation are justified as tools with which to slow such depletion and to hasten the development of technologies that would provide alternatives for future generations.

That argument is deeply problematic. Putting aside the issue of whether government as an institution has incentives to adopt a time horizon longer than that relevant for the private sector, the profit motive provides incentives for the market to consider the long-run effects of current decisions. The market rate of interest is a price that links the interests of generations present and future. If a resource is being depleted, then its expected future price will rise, other things held constant. If that rate of price increase is greater than the market interest rate, then owners of the resource have incentives to reduce production today—by doing so they can sell the resource in the future and in effect earn a rate of return higher than the market rate of interest—thus raising prices today and reducing expected future prices. In equilibrium, expected prices should rise at the market rate of interest, other factors held constant.[147] Under market institutions, it is the market rate of interest, again, that ties the interests of the current and future generations by making it profitable currently to conserve some considerable volume of exhaustible resources for future consumption.[148] Because of the market rate of interest, market forces will never allow the depletion of a given resource.

Accordingly, the market has powerful incentives to conserve, that is, to shift the consumption of large volumes of finite (or depletable) resources into future periods. That is why, for example, not all crude oil was used up decades ago even though the market price of crude oil always was greater than zero, which is to say that using it would have yielded value. In short, the "sustainability" argument for policy support for renewable electricity depends crucially on an assumption that the market conserves too little and that government has incentives to improve the allocation of exhaustible resources over time. That is a dual premise for which the underlying rationale is weak and for which little persuasive evidence has been presented.[149]

The Interests of Future Generations

The Obama administration argued that the use of an artificially low discount rate is an appropriate method to give sufficient weight to the interests of future generations, the members of which cannot vote now. Consider this formulation of that stance from the Council of Economic Advisers.

> The estimates of the cost of emissions released in a given year represent the present value of the additional damages that occur from those emissions between the year in which they are emitted and the year 2300. The choice of discount rate over such a long time horizon implicates philosophical and ethical perspectives about tradeoffs in consumption across generations, and debates about the appropriate discount rate in climate change analysis persist.[150]

Accordingly, we must ask whether an artificially low discount rate serves the interests of future generations. Consider a *Homo sapiens* baby borne in a cave some tens of thousands of years ago, in a world with a resource base virtually undiminished and environmental quality effectively untouched by mankind. That child at birth would have had a life expectancy on the order of 10 years; had it been able to choose, it is obvious that it willingly would have given up some resources and environmental quality in exchange for a longer life expectancy engendered by better housing, food, water, medical care, and safety, ad infinitum.[151] That is an illustration of the general proposition that people willingly give up some environmental quality in exchange for a life both longer and wealthier. Few would choose to live on a pristine desert island; most people prefer closer proximity to family, employment, entertainment, and all the other myriad dimensions of living.

In other words, the central interest of future generations in this context is a bequest from previous generations of the most valuable possible capital stock, of which the resource base and environmental quality are two important dimensions among many, and among which there always are trade-offs. That bequest preference on the part of future generations requires efficient resource allocation by the current generation. If regulatory and other policies implemented by the current generation yield less wealth currently and a smaller total capital stock for future generations, then, perhaps counterintuitively, some additional emissions of pollutants and GHG would be preferred (efficient) from the viewpoint of those future generations.[152] In short, enhanced environmental quality is only one objective pursued by individuals, whether already alive or yet to be born; accordingly, it is not appropriate to use an artificially low discount rate as a means of increasing the weight accorded the interests of future generations.

Arnold Harberger and Glenn Jenkins estimate "social discount rates of averaging around 8 percent for the advanced countries and 10 percent for healthy developing countries and Asian tigers."[153] James Broughel estimates a social discount rate of about 7 percent.[154] Robert Pindyck presents a useful summary and critique of the literature on this issue.[155] Juzhong Zhuang et al. present a useful summary of the older literature.[156] Note that Kenneth Arrow et al. argue that it would be efficient for government to use a declining discount rate in regulatory analysis.[157]

The Evidence on Climate Phenomena

The GND proponents justify their policy proposals as a response to a purported climate crisis, but it is difficult to find in their written and oral arguments a systematic summary of evidence in support of that general assertion. The latest evidence on climate phenomena can be summarized as follows.

Temperatures have been rising in fits and starts since 1850, roughly the end of the Little Ice Age (when the glaciers began to recede). The latest research suggests that mankind accounts for about half a degree of a total increase of about 1.5 degrees. Anthropogenic warming is not a "hoax."[158]

Sea levels have been rising for about 22,000 years and at a more or less constant rate for the past 8,000 years. The issue is whether the rise in sea levels has accelerated with increasing GHG concentrations, and on that the evidence is mixed. (The "yes" evidence is based on 17 years of data, which is not much to rely on in the context of climate phenomena.)[159]

The Arctic and Antarctic sea ice fluctuations tell very different stories, for reasons that "science" understands only poorly.[160] Tornado counts and intensities are either flat or declining since 1954.[161] Cyclone numbers and intensities have been flat or declining since the early 1970s.[162]

There has been no trend in the US wildfire data since 1985, despite increasing atmospheric concentrations of GHG.[163] Note that US Forest Service acreage in California is about 12 million acres, of which about three million is in congressional set-asides. Private forest acreage is about 8.5 million acres. For 2011–17, Forest Service acres burned in that state averaged about 378,000 acres, while the average for the private forests was about a third of that.[164] Such rough data are crude, but they do not support the argument of many that "climate change" is the cause of the wildfire problem. Is there a reason that increasing atmospheric concentrations of GHG should affect government forests disproportionately?

Drought shows no trend since 1895, and flooding is uncorrelated with increasing GHG concentrations.[165] The available data do not

Table 13. IPCC AR5 Climate System Projections

Climate System Effect	Likelihood	Confidence
Collapse of Atlantic Meridional Overturning Circulation	Very Unlikely	High
Ice Sheet Collapse	Exceptionally Unlikely	High
Permafrost Carbon Release	Possible	Low
Clathrate Methane Release	Very Unlikely	High
Tropical Forests Dieback		Low
Boreal Forests Dieback		Low
Disappearance of Summer Arctic Sea Ice	Likely Under RCP8.5	Medium
Long-Term Droughts		Low
Monsoonal Circulation Collapse		Low

Source: Thomas F. Stocker et al., *Climate Change 2013: The Physical Science Basis* (Cambridge, UK: Cambridge University Press, 2013), 1115, Table 12.4, https://www.ipcc.ch/report/ar5/wg1/.

support the ubiquitous assertions about the dire impacts of declining pH levels in the oceans.[166]

IPCC in the Fifth Assessment Report (AR5) is deeply dubious about the various extreme adverse effects of increasing GHG concentrations often asserted.[167] The only exception is the disappearance of the arctic summer sea ice, which IPCC views as "likely" with "medium confidence," but only under the extreme GHG scenario "Representative Concentration Pathway 8.5"(RCP8.5).[168] Table 13 summarizes the IPCC findings.

Perhaps evidence of serious climate impacts of increasing GHG concentrations will emerge over time as those concentrations rise further. Perhaps further analysis will suggest that the benefits of climate policies will exceed the costs. But simply to assume those conditions is a poor basis for policy formulation.

The Ontario Green Energy Act

In 2009, the Canadian province of Ontario implemented a Green Energy Act, which as a generalization was a much watered-down version of the GND.[169] Its central feature was implementation of a system of subsidized electricity purchase contracts for wind farms, solar panel installations, bioenergy producers, and small hydroelectric facilities. Those contracts guaranteed above-market prices for electricity produced by those facilities. According to a recent study by Ross McKitrick, one important goal was the closure of two coal-fired power plants. McKitrick has analyzed its effects; his summary findings are as follows.

- "It is unlikely the Green Energy Act will yield any environmental improvements other than those that would have happened anyway under policy and technology trends established since the 1970s. Indeed, it is plausible that adding more wind power to the grid will end up increasing overall air emissions from the power generation sector."

- "The plan implemented under the Green Energy Act is not cost effective. It is currently 10 times more costly than an alternative outlined in a confidential report to the government in 2005 that would have achieved the same environmental goals as closing the coal-fired power plants."

- "The Green Energy Act will not create jobs or improve economic growth in Ontario. Its overall effect will be to increase unit production costs, diminish competitiveness, cut the rate of return to capital in key sectors, reduce employment, and make households worse off." [170]

Ontario repealed the act in late 2018.[171]

8

Concluding Observations

The central premise of the GND is that a series of policies that would reduce sharply or destroy the economic value of some substantial part of the US resource base and the energy-producing and energy-consuming capital stock would increase the size of the economy in real terms, improve environmental quality, and improve distributional equity. This is not an argument to be taken seriously. Moreover, the central stated goal of the GND as an energy policy is amelioration of the purported "climate crisis." But the future temperature impacts of the zero-emissions objective would be close to zero.

And so a GND policy in its central energy and environment context would yield no benefits but impose large economic costs. The historical data on energy consumption and production, GDP growth, employment, rising incomes and energy consumption, and poverty make it clear that the GND would yield large adverse effects in each of those dimensions. In particular, because rising incomes result in greater energy consumption, parameters that have the effect of increasing incomes—education and health investment, technological advances, investments in productive plant and equipment, and so forth—are to be penalized precisely because the GND intellectual framework views greater energy consumption as a social "bad."

The electricity component of the GND is the least ambiguous. A highly conservative estimate of the aggregate cost of that set of policies would be $490.5 billion per year, permanently, or $3,845 per year per household. This would be accompanied by significant environmental damage—there is nothing clean about "clean" electricity—and massive land use. Without fossil-fired backup generation, another effect would be a significant decline in the reliability of the US electric power system—that is, a large increase in service interruptions. Other large costs would arise also, as hidden unintended consequences of the

Table 14. Annual Costs of the GND (Billions of 2018 Dollars)

GND Policy	Cost	Total Cost
Renewable Electricity Mandate		490
New Renewable Power Capacity	357	
Backup Capacity, Generation	76.9	
Emissions from Backup Generation	30.8	
Transmission	18	
Land	7.8	
Budget Cost of Forging a GND Political Coalition		4,000
Excess Burden of the Tax System		4,460
Annual Total		**8,950**

Source: Tables 10 and 11.

GND. Table 14 summarizes the cost findings reported above; a conservative estimate of the costs of the GND is about $9 trillion per year.

Note again that these figures do not include the massive costs of the shift away from fossil-fuel transportation, large-scale "high-speed rail," or the "efficiency" retrofit of every building in the country. Those GND proposals are far more ambiguous than the electricity dimension and thus lend themselves less to a rigorous cost analysis.[172] They also exclude adjustments for future economic growth and the resulting increase in the demand for energy, a reality that would increase the economic costs of a reduction in the supply of energy mandated by the GND. They exclude as well most of the economic costs of the adverse environmental effects of the GND electricity mandate and the costs of the inexorable increase in government authoritarianism attendant upon the GND, an effect difficult to measure but very real nonetheless.

The GND represents a massive increase in the power of government over the ability of individuals and businesses to use their resources in ways that they deem appropriate. As the adverse consequences of the GND emerge and grow, government inevitably will attempt to circumvent them by increasing the politicization of energy use, a process that inexorably will expand government surveillance of energy use and erode individual freedom and privacy.

The expansion of employment under the GND—in particular the expansion of "green" employment—will prove illusory. The resource "sustainability" rationale for the GND is fundamentally incorrect analytically. Future generations rationally would vote in favor of policies maximizing the value of the capital stock to be bequeathed to them; policies engendering massive resource waste by the current generation are inconsistent with that goal. The evidence on climate phenomena does not support the argument that a climate crisis is present or looming. And the experience of Ontario under its Green Energy Act should give pause to policymakers considering the GND policy proposals.

The GND at its core is the substitution of central planning in place of market forces for resource allocation, in the US energy and transportation sectors narrowly and in the broad industrial, business, and housing sectors writ large. Given the tragic and predictable record of central planning outcomes worldwide over the past century, the GND should be rejected.

Notes

1. See Recognizing the Duty of the Federal Government to Create a Green New Deal, H.R. 109, 116th Cong., 1st sess. (2019), https://www.congress.gov/116/bills/hres109/BILLS-116hres109ih.pdf (hereafter cited as H.R. 109). All of the following quotations come from this official resolution. See also Greg Carlock and Emily Mangan, *A Green New Deal: A Progressive Vision for Environmental Sustainability and Economic Stability*, Data for Progress, September 2018, https://static1.squarespace.com/static/5aa9be92f8370a24714de593/t/5ba14811032be48b8772d37e/1537296413290/GreenNewDeal_Final_v2_12MB.pdf. Another example is provided by the Green Party US, "Green New Deal—Full Language," http://www.gp.org/gnd_full. At the level of political coalition-building, see Sunrise Movement, https://www.sunrisemovement.org/.

2. See H.R. 109, 2–3.

3. See H.R. 109, 9.

4. See, for example, Roger O'Neill, "The Questionable Economic Feasibility of Carbon Capture Technology," Competitive Enterprise Institute, June 29, 2017, https://cei.org/blog/questionable-economic-feasibility-carbon-capture-technology; and Marlo Lewis Jr., "Carbon Capture and Storage Not 'Best System' to Reduce Emissions," Competitive Enterprise Institute, February 15, 2019, https://cei.org/blog/carbon-capture-and-storage-not-best-system-reduce-emissions.

5. See University Corporation for Atmospheric Research, "Model for the Assessment of Greenhouse-Gas Induced Climate Change: A Regional Climate Scenario Generator," http://www.cgd.ucar.edu/cas/wigley/magicc/.

6. Equilibrium climate sensitivity in simplest terms is the temperature effect of a doubling of atmospheric GHG concentrations after the climate system in total reaches a new equilibrium in response. For a discussion, see National Oceanographic and Atmospheric Administration, "Transient and Equilibrium Climate Sensitivity," https://www.gfdl.noaa.gov/transient-and-equilibrium-climate-sensitivity/. The Intergovernmental Panel on Climate Change (IPCC) in its Fifth Assessment Report provides a "likely" range (1.5°C to 4.5°C), the midpoint of which is 3°C. See Lisa V. Alexander et al., "Summary for Policymakers," in *Climate Change 2013: The Physical Science Basis*, ed. Thomas F. Stocker et al. (Cambridge, UK: Cambridge University

Press, 2013), 23, Table SPM.2, http://www.climatechange2013.org/images/
report/WG1AR5_SPM_FINAL.pdf. The latest research published in the peer-
reviewed literature suggests a figure below 2°C. See Patrick J. Michaels, "At
What Cost? Examining the Social Cost of Carbon," statement before the Subcommittee on Environment and Subcommittee on Oversight, Committee
on Science, Space, and Technology, US House of Representatives, February
28, 2017, https://www.cato.org/publications/testimony/what-cost-examining-
social-cost-carbon. See also Nicholas Lewis and Judith Curry, "The Impact of
Recent Forcing and Ocean Heat Uptake Data on Estimates of Climate Sensitivity," *Journal of Climate* 31, no. 15 (August 2018): 6051–71, https://journals.
ametsoc.org/doi/abs/10.1175/JCLI-D-17-0667.1; John R. Christy and Richard T.
McNider, "Satellite Bulk Tropospheric Temperatures as a Metric for Climate
Sensitivity," *Asia-Pacific Journal of Atmospheric Science* 53, no. 4 (2017): 511–18,
https://wattsupwiththat.files.wordpress.com/2017/11/2017_christy_mcnider-1.
pdf; and Ross McKitrick and John Christy, "A Test of the Tropical 200- to
300-hPa Warming Rate in Climate Models," *Earth and Space Science* 5 (2018),
https://agupubs.onlinelibrary.wiley.com/doi/full/10.1029/2018EA000401.

7. See James Hansen et al., "GISS Analysis of Surface Temperature
Change," *Journal of Geophysical Research* 104, no. D24 (December 27, 1999): 30997–
1022, https://agupubs.onlinelibrary.wiley.com/doi/pdf/10.1029/1999JD900835.

8. For example, see Lisa V. Alexander et al., "Summary for Policymakers,"
in *Climate Change 2013: The Physical Science Basis*, ed. Thomas F. Stocker et al.
(Cambridge, UK: Cambridge University Press, 2013), 21, Figure SPM.7, http://
www.climatechange2013.org/images/report/WG1AR5_SPM_FINAL.pdf.

9. Consider the case of former EPA administrator Gina McCarthy during
a 2013 hearing before the House Energy and Commerce Committee. When
asked by then-Rep. Mike Pompeo (R-KS) about the estimated climate impacts
of the Obama Climate Action Plan regulatory effort, McCarthy did not answer
the question, instead asserting that the existing and proposed regulatory
effort "is part of an overall strategy that is positioning the U.S. for leadership
in an international discussion." See Marlo Lewis, "Rep. Pompeo Questions
EPA Administrator McCarthy on Obama Climate Plan," GlobalWarming.org,
September 18, 2013, http://www.globalwarming.org/2013/09/18/rep-pompeo-
questions-epa-administrator-mccarthy-on-obama-climate-plan/. For a discussion of the policy implications of the IPCC GHG scenarios, see Benjamin
Zycher, "The Climate Empire Strikes Out: The Perils of Policy Analysis in an

Echo Chamber," *American Enterprise Institute*, September 26, 2018, https://www.aei.org/publication/the-climate-empire-strikes-out-the-perils-of-policy-analysis-in-an-echo-chamber/.

10. See comments by Rep. Kathy Castor (D-FL), newly named chairman of the House Select Committee on the Climate Crisis, as quoted in Chris Mills Rodrigo, "Pelosi Names Castor Chair of Select Committee on Climate Crisis," *Hill*, December 28, 2018, https://thehill.com/homenews/house/423120-pelosi-names-castor-chair-of-select-committee-on-climate-crisis.

11. See endnote 9; and UN Framework Convention on Climate Change, "Conference of the Parties (COP)," https://unfccc.int/process/bodies/supreme-bodies/conference-of-the-parties-cop.

12. See H.R. 109, 3.

13. The Paris agreement, if implemented immediately and enforced strictly, would reduce temperatures in 2100 by 0.17°C. Benjamin Zycher, "The Climate Empire Strikes Out: The Perils of Policy Analysis in an Echo Chamber," *American Enterprise Institute*, September 26, 2018, Table 3, https://www.aei.org/publication/the-climate-empire-strikes-out-the-perils-of-policy-analysis-in-an-echo-chamber/. See also Benjamin Zycher, "Saving the Planet: How Climate Breakthroughs Are Made," *InsideSources*, December 14, 2015, https://www.insidesources.com/saving-the-planet-how-climate-breakthroughs-are-made/; and Benjamin Zycher, "Paris in the Fall: COP-21 vs Climate Evidence," *American Enterprise Institute*, November 30, 2015, http://www.aei.org/publication/paris-in-the-fall-cop-21-vs-climate-evidence/.

14. Note, however, that the narrowly environmental or climate goals of the GND would have substantial social impacts in terms of reduced national wealth and employment, direct or indirect changes in land-use patterns and business and household location decisions, and a multitude of other such parameters. Some of these are discussed in Chapters 2–6.

15. In economic terminology, such a policy would shift the "production possibilities frontier" for the US economy inward, thus reducing the value of aggregate output even if all remaining resources and capital were employed efficiently. This ignores the possible economic damage caused by increasing atmospheric concentrations of GHG, but as discussed in Chapter 7, there is little evidence of a climate crisis defined in terms of such serious impacts. Moreover, there also is possible an array of benefits from an earth warming due to anthropogenic effects, particularly in the likely event of a future glaciation,

whether or not distant in time. See, for example, the time series "greening" photos of the earth published by NASA: Samson Reiny, "CO_2 Is Making Earth Greener—for Now," National Aeronautics and Space Administration, April 26, 2016, https://climate.nasa.gov/news/2436/co2-is-making-earth-greenerfor-now/. Moreover, government policy always carries the prospect of adverse impacts, however unintended or unforeseen. Note that "the value of aggregate output" conceptually is driven by individual preferences as reflected in market prices; this definition is normative, in that one might reject individual preferences as the determinants of "value" on various grounds. That is, there is nothing "scientific" about the concept of "economic value" defined in terms of individual preferences. However, arguments against defining "value" as the result of individual preferences implicitly must reject the freedom of individuals to use their resources and to engage in voluntary transactions as they deem appropriate. In that conceptual framework, market prices do not reflect marginal value. The existence of externalities often is used as a rationale for rejecting market prices as a measure of value, but that set of arguments is deeply problematic. See, for example, Harold Demsetz, "The Problem of Social Cost: What Problem?," *Review of Law & Economics* 7, no. 1 (2011): 1–13; Steven N. S. Cheung, "The Myth of Social Cost," Cato Institute, 1980; Carl J. Dahlman, "The Problem of Externality," *Journal of Law and Economics* 22, no. 1 (April 1979): 141–62; and Ryan Bourne, "How 'Market Failure' Arguments Lead to Misguided Policy," Cato Institute, January 22, 2019, https://object.cato.org/sites/cato.org/files/pubs/pdf/pa-863.pdf. See also Donald Boudreaux and Roger Meiners, "Externality: Origins and Classifications," *Natural Resources Journal*, forthcoming in 2019. Chapter 7 discusses briefly the available evidence on the "crisis" view of the purported GHG externality. Moreover, replacement of market prices as an allocational mechanism for resource use with some other system is certain to yield its own set of "externalities" engendered by the political reward/penalty framework driving policy decision-making. That other framework by definition would be heavily politicized; it is difficult to believe that government policymaking is driven by a set of incentives yielding "efficiency." See, for example, Dennis C. Mueller, *Public Choice III* (Cambridge, UK: University of Cambridge, 2003), 333–405; William A. Niskanen, "Bureaucrats and Politicians," *Journal of Law and Economics* 18, no. 3 (December 1975): 617–43; Kelly H. Chang et al., "Rational Choice Theories of Bureaucratic Control and Performance," in *The Elgar Companion to Public Choice*, ed. William F. Shughart

II and Laura Razzolini (Northampton, UK: Edward Elgar, 2001); and Randall G. Holcombe, *An Advanced Introduction to Public Choice* (Northampton, UK: Edward Elgar, 2016), 63–72. See also James M. Buchanan, *Demand and Supply of Public Goods* (Chicago: Rand McNally, 1968), 127–49; and Bryan Ellickson, "A Generalization of the Pure Theory of Public Goods," *American Economic Review* 63, no. 3 (June 1973): 417–32.

16. For purposes of this discussion, I have shunted aside obvious endogeneity issues, missing variables problems, and the effects of outliers, which normally would be mandatory for a research paper, but which are beside the point for the purposes served here. Correlations obviously are not direct evidence of causation, but the simple correlations presented here are meaningful in that they are both strong and consistent with a sensible economic model, in that it is not plausible that, for example, the correlation between GDP growth and changes in energy consumption is spurious. The data suggest strongly that an expansion of energy supplies—the horizontal drilling and fracking revolution is a good example—would be salutary for output and employment and that the opposite is true for the energy supply and consumption constraints that are central to the GND.

17. See Benjamin Zycher, *Renewable Electricity Generation: Economic Analysis and Outlook* (Washington DC: AEI Press, 2011), http://www.aei.org/publication/renewable-electricity-generation/.

18. For US energy consumption and production, see US Energy Information Administration, Total Energy, https://www.eia.gov/totalenergy/data/browser/index.php?tbl=T01.01#/?f=M. For US GDP, see US Bureau of Economic Analysis, National Data, https://apps.bea.gov/iTable/iTable.cfm?reqid=19&step=2#reqid=19&step=2&isuri=1&1921=survey. Correlations and percent changes in the two series were computed by the author.

19. US Energy Information Administration, Total Energy, https://www.eia.gov/totalenergy/data/browser/index.php?tbl=T01.01#/?f=M; and US Bureau of Economic Analysis, National Data, https://apps.bea.gov/iTable/iTable.cfm?reqid=19&step=2#reqid=19&step=2&isuri=1&1921=survey.

20. Note that "energy efficiency" is not the same as "economic efficiency." Reductions in energy use driven by, say, regulatory requirements, which would not be observed merely as a result of shifts driven by market prices, may be inefficient economically—that is, more costly than justified by narrow economic considerations, unless the regulatory constraints yield resource

allocation more productive in the aggregate due, for example, to improved environmental quality worth more than the costs in terms of other forgone output. The issue of whether regulatory processes are likely to yield efficient outcomes is outside the focus here, but see the references cited in endnote 15. The usual justifications offered for the energy policies observed since the 1970s analytically are vastly weaker than commonly assumed. See Benjamin Zycher, "Four Decades of Subsidy Rationales for Uncompetitive Energy," statement before the Committee on Finance, US Senate, June 14, 2016, https://www.finance.senate.gov/imo/media/doc/14jun2016Zycher.pdf.

21. Annual nonfarm employment data are from Federal Reserve Bank of St. Louis, FRED, s.v. "All Employees: Total Nonfarm Payrolls," https://fred.stlouisfed.org/series/PAYEMS. Energy consumption data are from US Energy Information Administration, Total Energy, https://www.eia.gov/totalenergy/data/browser/index.php?tbl=T01.01#/?f=M .

22. This observation applies to a reduction in energy costs resulting from an outward supply shift, the opposite of the supply reduction proposed as the central feature of the GND. A reduction in energy demand resulting, say, from a downturn in economic activity would reduce both energy prices and employment.

23. Employment data are from Federal Reserve Bank of St. Louis, FRED, s.v. "All Employees: Total Nonfarm Payrolls," https://fred.stlouisfed.org/series/PAYEMS. Energy consumption data are from US Energy Information Administration, Total Energy, https://www.eia.gov/totalenergy/data/browser/index.php?tbl=T01.01#/?f=M .

24. See US Bureau of Labor Statistics, Consumer Expenditure Survey, https://www.bls.gov/cex/ and https://beta.bls.gov/dataQuery/find?st=18000&r=100&s=title%3AA&fq=survey:[cx]&more=0. For all households and for Quintiles I, II, III, IV, and V, respectively, average household incomes before taxes in 2017 were $73,573, $11,394, $29,821, $52,431, $86,363, and $188,103. The large increase from Quintile IV to Quintile V is explained by the absence of an upper bound on the latter. See US Bureau of Labor Statistics, Data Finder, https://beta.bls.gov/dataQuery/find?st=400&r=100&s=title%3AA&q=income+quintiles&more=0. The expenditure data were deflated by the author to 2017 dollars using the data reported by the US Bureau of Economic Analysis for the implicit price deflator for personal consumption expenditures, as detailed by the Federal Reserve Bank of St. Louis, FRED, s.v. "Personal Consumption Expenditures (Implicit Price Deflator)," https://fred.stlouisfed.org/series/DPCERD3A086NBEA.

25. See endnote 15. See also Alex Epstein, *The Moral Case for Fossil Fuels* (New York: Penguin, 2014), 37–63; and Michael R. Strain and Stan Veuger, eds., *Economic Freedom and Human Flourishing: Perspectives from Political Philosophy* (Washington, DC: AEI Press, 2016), 96–149.

26. I shunt aside here the problems with the calculation of the official poverty rate. For discussions, see, for example, Bruce D. Meyer and James X. Sullivan, "Annual Report on US Consumption Poverty: 2017," American Enterprise Institute, October 31, 2018, https://www.aei.org/wp-content/uploads/2018/11/2017-Consumption-Poverty-Report-Meyer-Sullivan-final.pdf; and John F. Early, "Reassessing the Facts About Inequality, Poverty, and Redistribution," Cato Institute, April 24, 2018, https://object.cato.org/sites/cato.org/files/pubs/pdf/pa-839-updated-2.pdf.

27. See US Energy Information Administration, Total Energy, https://www.eia.gov/totalenergy/data/browser/index.php?tbl=T01.01#/?f=M; Kayla Fontenot, Jessica Semega, and Melissa Kollar, "Income and Poverty in the United States: 2017," US Bureau of the Census, September 12, 2018, https://www.census.gov/library/publications/2018/demo/p60-263.html; and US Bureau of the Census, "Impact on Poverty of Alternative Resource Measure by Age: 1981 to 2017," September 2018, https://www2.census.gov/programs-surveys/demo/tables/p60/263/Impact_Poverty.xls.

28. Figure 7 shows the annual percent changes; Figure 8 shows the annual absolute changes, or differences.

29. US Energy Information Administration, *State Energy Production Estimates 1960 Through 2016*, 2018, https://www.eia.gov/state/seds/sep_prod/SEDS_Production_Report.pdf; US Census Bureau, "Table H-8. Median Household Income by State: 1984 to 2017," 2018, https://www2.census.gov/programs-surveys/cps/tables/time-series/historical-income-households/h08.xls; US Census Bureau, "Historical Poverty Tables: People and Families—1959 to 2017," August 28, 2018, https://www.census.gov/data/tables/time-series/demo/income-poverty/historical-poverty-people.html; National Center for Education Statistics, "Digest of Education Statistics: 2007," Table 20, https://nces.ed.gov/programs/digest/d07/tables/dt07_020.asp; US Bureau of Labor Statistics, Local Area Unemployment Statistics, https://www.bls.gov/lau/lastrk17.htm; and Iowa State University, "Annual Unemployment Rates by State," https://www.icip.iastate.edu/tables/employment/unemployment-states.

30. I shunt aside here the issue of whether there occurred changes in the

sizes and other characteristics of US households. Census Bureau data show that for the US as a whole, average household size declined from 2.62 persons in 2000 to 2.54 in 2017. See US Census Bureau, Historical Households Tables, November 2018, Table HH-6, https://www.census.gov/data/tables/time-series/demo/families/households.html.

31. See, for example, Nicolas Loris, "Ethanol and Biofuel Policies," Downsizing the Federal Government, February 9, 2017, https://www.downsizinggovernment.org/ethanol-and-biofuel-policies.

32. This allocational (or "structural") shift of labor resources across sectors might be offset by the employment of labor resources previously unemployed, but differing demands and supplies of given skills might make the use of unemployed labor problematic, at least in the short run.

33. See H.R. 9, 12.

34. Note again that the trivial climate or environmental effects of the net-zero GHG goal mean that the magnitude of environmental benefits, however difficult to measure, would not compensate for the explicit reduction in economic output and incomes. This conclusion would not change were I to include assumed "co-benefit" reductions in emissions of other pollutants correlated with emissions of GHG, unless I assume that the emissions requirements specified in the Clean Air Act are inefficiently lax, the implementation of those requirements has failed to achieve them, or it somehow is appropriate to drive such emissions down to levels at which the marginal benefits are exceeded by the marginal costs.

35. See Tyler Cowen, "Public Goods and Externalities," in *The Concise Encyclopedia of Economics*, ed. David Henderson (Indianapolis, IN: Library of Economics and Liberty, 2002), http://www.econlib.org/library/Enc1/PublicGoodsandExternalities.html. A "technological" externality is what most references to "externalities" mean. There also are "pecuniary" externalities, for example, the price-increase effects of an increase in the demand for a good. In general, pecuniary externalities do not create allocational inefficiencies in the standard model. See Dean A. Worcester Jr., "Pecuniary and Technological Externality, Factor Rents, and Social Costs," *American Economic Review* 59, no. 5 (December 1969): 873–85, https://www.jstor.org/stable/1810682.

36. This is "excessive" only in the context of individual preferences, such that an increase in the value of aggregate output could be effected. See endnote 15.

37. See Ronald Coase, "The Problem of Social Cost," *Journal of Law & Economics* 3 (October 1960): 1–44. See also endnote 15.

38 See endnote 15.

39. See Executive Office of the President, "The President's Climate Action Plan," June 2013, https://obamawhitehouse.archives.gov/sites/default/files/image/president27sclimateactionplan.pdf.

40. See Interagency Working Group on Social Cost of Greenhouse Gases, "Technical Support Document: Technical Update of the Social Cost of Carbon for Regulatory Impact Analysis Under Executive Order 12866," August 2016, https://obamawhitehouse.archives.gov/sites/default/files/omb/inforeg/scc_tsd_final_clean_8_26_16.pdf.

41. See Benjamin Zycher, "The Social Cost of Carbon, Greenhouse Gas Policies, and Politicized Benefit/Cost Analysis," *Texas A&M Law Review* 6, no. 1 (2018): 59–76, https://scholarship.law.tamu.edu/cgi/viewcontent.cgi?article=1154&context=lawreview. For the Administrative Procedures Act, see US Department of Justice, "Administrative Procedure Act (P.L. 79-404)," July 10, 2015, https://www.justice.gov/jmd/ls/administrative-procedure-act-pl-79-404.

42. For the regulatory impact analysis for the Clean Power Plan, see US Environmental Protection Agency, *Regulatory Impact Analysis for the Clean Power Plan Final Rule,* October 23, 2015, https://www3.epa.gov/ttnecas1/docs/ria/utilities_ria_final-clean-power-plan-existing-units_2015-08.pdf.

43. See US Environmental Protection Agency, *Regulatory Impact Analysis for the Clean Power Plan Final Rule,* October 23, 2015, p. ES-22, Table ES-9, footnote d, and p. ES-23, Table ES-10, footnote d, https://www3.epa.gov/ttnecas1/docs/ria/utilities_ria_final-clean-power-plan-existing-units_2015-08.pdf. Another example of the analytic machinations underlying the Obama administration climate regulations is provided by the proposed "efficiency" rule for medium and heavy trucks. In the regulatory impact analysis for that rule, the Obama administration estimated that the regulation would reduce temperatures in 2100 by between 0.0026 and 0.0065 of a degree, an effect that was asserted to yield net economic benefits of over $100 billion. See Environmental Protection Agency, "Greenhouse Gas Emissions and Fuel Efficiency Standards for Medium and Heavy-Duty Engines and Vehicles; Phase 2," July 13, 2015, Table VII-37 and Section I.D, https://www.regulations.gov/document?D=EPA-HQ-OAR-2014-0827-0002. See also Benjamin Zycher, "The Social Cost of Carbon, Greenhouse Gas Policies, and Politicized Benefit/Cost Analysis,"

Texas A&M Law Review 6, no. 1 (2018): 59–76, https://scholarship.law.tamu.edu/cgi/viewcontent.cgi?article=1154&context=lawreview.

44. See Richard S. J. Tol, "The Private Benefit of Carbon and Its Social Cost" (working paper, University of Sussex, 2017), https://www.sussex.ac.uk/webteam/gateway/file.php?name=wps-07-2017.pdf&site=24.

45. See Interagency Working Group on Social Cost of Greenhouse Gases, "Technical Support Document: Technical Update of the Social Cost of Carbon for Regulatory Impact Analysis Under Executive Order 12866," August 2016, Table ES-1, https://obamawhitehouse.archives.gov/sites/default/files/omb/inforeg/scc_tsd_final_clean_8_26_16.pdf.

46. See US Environmental Protection Agency, *Inventory of U.S. Greenhouse Gas Emissions and Sinks: 1990–2016*, ES-4, Figure ES-1, https://www.epa.gov/sites/production/files/2018-01/documents/2018_executive_summary.pdf.

47. See Travis Fisher and Alex Fitzsimmons, "Big Wind's Dirty Little Secret: Toxic Lakes and Radioactive Waste," Institute for Energy Research, October 23, 2013, https://www.instituteforenergyresearch.org/renewable/wind/big-winds-dirty-little-secret-rare-earth-minerals/.

48. See Anabela Botelho et al., "Effect of Wind Farm Noise on Local Residents' Decision to Adopt Mitigation Measures," *International Journal of Environmental Research and Public Health* 14, no. 7 (July 2017), https://www.ncbi.nlm.nih.gov/pmc/articles/PMC5551191/pdf/ijerph-14-00753.pdf; and Loren D. Knopper et al., "Wind Turbines and Human Health," *Frontiers in Public Health* 2 (June 2014): 1–20, https://www.ncbi.nlm.nih.gov/pmc/articles/PMC4063257/pdf/fpubh-02-00063.pdf.

49. See Institute for Energy Research, "The Mounting Solar Panel Waste Problem," September 12, 2018, https://www.instituteforenergyresearch.org/renewable/solar/the-mounting-solar-panel-waste-problem/; Dustin Mulvaney, "Solar Energy Isn't Always as Green as You Think," *IEEE Spectrum*, November 13, 2014, https://spectrum.ieee.org/green-tech/solar/solar-energy-isnt-always-as-green-as-you-think; and Institute for Energy Research, "Will Solar Power Be at Fault for the Next Environmental Crisis?," August 15, 2017, https://www.instituteforenergyresearch.org/uncategorized/will-solar-power-fault-next-environmental-crisis/.

50. See Travis Fisher and Alex Fitzsimmons, "'Cuisinarts of the Sky' Continue to Dodge Environmental Laws," Institute for Energy Research, October 16, 2013, https://www.instituteforenergyresearch.org/renewable/wind/

cuisinarts-of-the-sky-continue-to-dodge-environmental-laws/; and Rebecca A. Kagan et al., "Avian Mortality at Solar Energy Facilities in Southern California: A Preliminary Analysis," https://alternativeenergy.procon.org/sourcefiles/avian-mortality-solar-energy-ivanpah-apr-2014.pdf.

51. For a discussion, see Vaclav Smil, *Energy at the Crossroads* (Cambridge, MA: MIT Press, 2003), 125–28. Note that this does not mean that wind generation is economic at 10–20 percent or less of total system generation; it means only that the wind generation tends not to impose higher system intermittency costs relative to the unexpected outage costs associated with conventional capacity. It still may be higher cost for other reasons, and as discussed below, the power produced by wind capacity is likely to be worth less than the power produced by dispatchable units because of the inverse correlation between wind strength and peak demands, both daily and seasonal.

52. See Seth Blumsack, "Frequency Regulation," Pennsylvania State University, https://www.e-education.psu.edu/ebf483/node/705; and US Department of Energy, *2017 Wind Technologies Market Report*, August 2018, 38, Figure 33, https://www.energy.gov/sites/prod/files/2018/08/f54/2017_wind_technologies_market_report_8.15.18.v2.pdf.

53. See Mark Z. Jacobson et al., "100% Clean and Renewable Wind, Water, and Sunlight All-Sector Energy Roadmaps for 139 Countries of the World," *Joule* 1, no. 1 (September 6, 2017): 108–21, https://www.sciencedirect.com/science/article/pii/S2542435117300120?via%3Dihub.

54. Christopher T. M. Clack et al., "Evaluation of a Proposal for Reliable Low-Cost Grid Power with 100% Wind, Water, and Solar," *Proceedings of the National Academy of Sciences* 114, no. 26 (June 27, 2017), https://www.pnas.org/content/pnas/114/26/6722.full.pdf; and Christopher T. M. Clack et al., "Supporting Information for the Paper 'Evaluation of a Proposal for Reliable Low-Cost Grid Power with 100% Wind, Water, and Solar,'" *Proceedings of the National Academy of Sciences* 30, no. 20 (May 8, 2017): 1–13, https://www.pnas.org/content/pnas/suppl/2017/06/16/1610381114.DCSupplemental/pnas.1610381114.sapp.pdf. See also Steve Huntoon, "Alternative Facts and Global Warming," *RTO Insider*, August 8, 2017, http://www.energy-counsel.com/docs/Alternative-Facts-and-Global-Warming.pdf; and Robert Blohm, "The Green New Deal's Impossible Electric Grid," *Wall Street Journal*, February 20, 2019, https://www.wsj.com/articles/the-green-new-deals-impossible-electric-grid-11550705997.

55. See Elena Verdolini, Francesco Vona, and David Popp, "Bridging the

Gap: Do Fast-Reacting Fossil Technologies Facilitate Renewable Energy Diffusion?," *Energy Policy* 116 (May 2018): 242–56, https://www.sciencedirect.com/science/article/pii/S0301421518300685.

56. Larry D. Hamlin (former vice president for power production, Southern California Edison Co., and former California Electricity Construction Czar), in discussion with the author, February 12, 2019. See also US Department of Energy, *2017 Wind Technologies Market Report*, August 2018, https://www.energy.gov/sites/prod/files/2018/08/f54/2017_wind_technologies_market_report_8.15.18.v2.pdf; and Philip Heptonstall, Robert Gross, and Florian Steiner, "The Costs and Impacts of Intermittency—2016 Update," UK Energy Research Centre, February 2017, http://www.ukerc.ac.uk/publications/the-costs-and-impacts-of-intermittency-2016-update.html. I assume here for simplicity that the dispatchable backup capacity would be gas combined cycle, in that nuclear units cannot be cycled up and down for technical reasons.

57. The discussion above of the direct environmental damage caused by wind and solar power is wholly qualitative; it does not quantify it in economic terms. The figures in Table 2 are the economic costs (using the Obama administration's calculation of the social cost of carbon) of the emissions resulting from the backup generation necessary to avoid service interruptions.

58. See Interagency Working Group on Social Cost of Greenhouse Gases, "Technical Support Document: Technical Update of the Social Cost of Carbon for Regulatory Impact Analysis Under Executive Order 12866," August 2016, https://obamawhitehouse.archives.gov/sites/default/files/omb/inforeg/scc_tsd_final_clean_8_26_16.pdf; and Benjamin Zycher, "The Social Cost of Carbon, Greenhouse Gas Policies, and Politicized Benefit/Cost Analysis," *Texas A&M Law Review* 6, no. 1 (2018): 59–76, https://scholarship.law.tamu.edu/cgi/viewcontent.cgi?article=1154&context=lawreview.

59. See Benjamin Zycher, "Observations on Volume 2 of the Fourth National Climate Assessment," American Enterprise Institute, November 29, 2018, http://www.aei.org/publication/observations-on-volume-2-of-the-fourth-national-climate-assessment/.

60. See Benjamin Zycher, "The Social Cost of Carbon, Greenhouse Gas Policies, and Politicized Benefit/Cost Analysis," *Texas A&M Law Review* 6, no. 1 (2018): 59–76, https://scholarship.law.tamu.edu/cgi/viewcontent.cgi?article=1154&context=lawreview.

61. As shown in Zycher, "The Social Cost of Carbon," small changes in only

one parameter—the discount rate—reduces the SCC in the Obama analysis to a figure close to zero, even apart from all the other problems inherent in that Obama SCC analysis. See endnote 41.

62. See Tables 3 and 5; US Energy Information Administration, *Electric Power Annual 2017*, December 2018, Table 8.2, https://www.eia.gov/electricity/annual/html/epa_08_02.html; US Energy Information Administration, "Natural Gas Consumption by End Use," February 28, 2019, https://www.eia.gov/dnav/ng/ng_cons_sum_dcu_nus_a.htm; US Energy Information Administration, *February 2019 Monthly Energy Review*, February 25, 2019, 209, Table 12.6, https://www.eia.gov/totalenergy/data/monthly/pdf/sec12_9.pdf; Interagency Working Group on Social Cost of Greenhouse Gases, "Technical Support Document: Technical Update of the Social Cost of Carbon for Regulatory Impact Analysis Under Executive Order 12866," August 2016, https://obamawhitehouse.archives.gov/sites/default/files/omb/inforeg/scc_tsd_final_clean_8_26_16.pdf; Gabriel Leon and Lourdes Mendoza Gonzalez, "Heat Rate Curve and Breakeven Point Model for Combine Cycle Gas Turbine Plants," ResearchGate, August 2018, Figure 10, https://www.researchgate.net/publication/327059862_Heat_rate_curve_and_breakeven_point_model_for_combine_cycle_gas_turbine_plants; and author's computations.

63. Some examples of the literature relevant to the backup emissions implications of large expansions of renewable electricity are Antonio Cardoso Marques et al., "Have Fossil Fuels Been Substituted by Renewables? An Empirical Assessment for 10 European Countries," *Energy Policy* 116 (May 2018): 257–65, https://www.sciencedirect.com/science/article/pii/S0301421518300983?via%3Dihub; Kent Hawkins, "Wind Integration: Incremental Emissions from Back-Up Generation Cycling," MasterResource, February 12, 2010, parts I–V, http://www.masterresource.org/2010/02/wind-integration-incremental-emissions-from-back-up-generation-cycling-part-v-calculator-update/; Charles R. Frank Jr., *The Net Benefits of Low and No-Carbon Electricity Technologies*, Brookings Institution, May 2014, https://www.brookings.edu/wp-content/uploads/2016/06/Net-Benefits-Final.pdf; James L. Plummer et al., "U.S. Wind and Solar Are Much Less Efficient Decarbonizers Than Combined Cycle Gas Turbines," National Wind Watch, January 8, 2018, https://www.wind-watch.org/documents/wind-and-solar-are-much-less-efficient-decarbonizers-than-combined-cycle-gas-turbines/; Bentek Energy, *The Wind Power Paradox*, July 2011, https://www.lsarc.ca/BENTEK_Wind_Power_Paradox.pdf; Bentek

Energy, *How Less Became More: Wind, Power and Unintended Consequences in the Colorado Energy Market*, April 16, 2010, https://docs.wind-watch.org/BENTEK-How-Less-Became-More.pdf; and Joseph Cullen, "Measuring the Environmental Benefits of Wind-Generated Electricity," *American Economic Journal: Economic Policy* 5, no. 4 (November 2013): 107–33, https://www.aeaweb.org/articles?id=10.1257/pol.5.4.107. See also the references linked in John Droz Jr., "Some Misc Wind Energy Realities," March 10, 2019, http://wiseenergy.org/Energy/Wind_Other/Wind_Energy_Realities.pdf.

64. The GDP data are available from the Federal Reserve Bank of St. Louis, FRED database, s.v. "Gross Domestic Product," https://fred.stlouisfed.org/tags/series?t=gdp.

65. In the context of current forecasts, that 3 percent growth assumption is optimistic. See Federal Reserve Bank of St. Louis, "FOMC Summary of Economic Projections for the Growth Rate of Real Gross Domestic Product, Central Tendency, Midpoint," https://fred.stlouisfed.org/series/GDPC1CTM. Note, however, that economic forecasting is hardly "science," and forecasts of GDP growth rates are notorious for their unreliability. See Allan H. Meltzer, "Limits of Short-Run Stabilization Policy Presidential Address to the Western Economic Association, July 3, 1986," *Economic Inquiry* 25, no 1 (January 1987): 1–14, https://onlinelibrary.wiley.com/doi/abs/10.1111/j.1465-7295.1987.tb00718.x.

66. But see the discussion in Chapter 2.

67. For a useful summary discussion and review of the literature, see Richard T. Carson, "The Environmental Kuznets Curve: Seeking Empirical Regularity and Theoretical Structure," *Review of Environmental Economics and Policy* 4, no. 1 (Winter 2010): 3–23, https://econweb.ucsd.edu/~rcarson/papers/Reep2010.pdf.

68. Even the political leadership in autocracies must satisfy the demands of some set of interests. See Gordon Tullock, *Autocracy* (Boston: Kluwer Academic Publishers, 1987), 17–33.

69. See endnote 1; and Saikat Chakrabarti, "Overview," https://assets.documentcloud.org/documents/5729035/Green-New-Deal-FAQ.pdf. The terms "renewable" and "nonrenewable" are somewhat misleading; it is clear that what proponents of unconventional power technologies actually mean by "renewable" is "non-depletable," that is, that fossil and nuclear fuels are finite in terms of physical availability, cannot be replaced physically, and so pose a prospect of physical exhaustion, unlike the case for wind flows and sunlight.

That argument is fundamentally flawed: Given enforceable property rights in "depletable" resources, market forces driven by price expectations and the market rate of interest will never allow the depletion of a finite resource; instead, the expected dynamic price path (or, more specifically, the path of economic returns to holding inventories of the finite resource) will rise at a rate equal to the market rate of interest. Price is a reasonable proxy for that economic return. See Benjamin Zycher, *Renewable Electricity Generation: Economic Analysis and Outlook* (Washington DC: AEI Press, 2011), http://www.aei.org/publication/renewable-electricity-generation; and Benjamin Zycher, "World Oil Prices: Market Expectations, the House of Saud, and the Transient Effect of Supply Disruptions," American Enterprise Institute, June 2016, http://www.aei.org/wp-content/uploads/2016/06/World-Oil-Prices.pdf. Moreover, most of the resources used to transform wind flows and sunlight into electricity are depletable—that is, physically limited in quantity—as well.

70. US Energy Information Administration, *Electric Power Annual* (data for 2017), October 22, 2018, Table 4.3, https://www.eia.gov/electricity/annual/html/epa_04_03.html.

71. As of the time that this report is being written, the various GND proposals vary in terms of which power technologies would qualify as "renewable" or "clean." H.R. 109 mentions neither nuclear nor hydroelectric power either positively or negatively. Carlock and Mangan state that neither power technology would be replaced in their version of the GND: "All electricity consumed in America must be generated by renewable sources, including solar, wind, hydro, geothermal, sustainable biomass, and renewable natural gas, as well as clean sources such as nuclear and remaining fossil fuel with carbon capture." Greg Carlock and Emily Mangan, *A Green New Deal: A Progressive Vision for Environmental Sustainability and Economic Stability*, Data for Progress, September 2018, https://static1.squarespace.com/static/5aa9be92f8370a24714de593/t/5ba14811032be48b8772d37e/1537296413290/GreenNewDeal_Final_v2_12MB.pdf. But the letter to Congress endorsed by 626 organizations states that "in addition to excluding fossil fuels, any definition of renewable energy must also exclude all combustion-based power generation, nuclear, biomass energy, large-scale hydro and waste-to-energy technologies." See Earthworks et al., "Legislation to Address the Urgent Threat of Climate Change," January 10, 2019, https://earthworks.org/cms/assets/uploads/2019/01/Green-New-Deal-ltr-to-Congress-20190110.pdf. I have defined "renewable" power for the analytic

purposes here as excluding nuclear technologies but including hydroelectric power, essentially because an effort as envisioned in a GND to replace nuclear power is feasible, however costly, while I believe that an effort to eliminate hydroelectric facilities would be essentially impossible. However, I assume also that no new hydroelectric capacity would be built to replace conventional capacity phased out as a result of GND policies. The replacement capacity is assumed here to comprise only wind and solar technologies, in a 2:1 ratio by capacity.

72. US Energy Information Administration, *Electric Power Annual* (data for 2017), October 22, 2018, Tables 3.1.A and 3.1.B, https://www.eia.gov/electricity/annual/html/epa_04_03.html.

73. For solar power, see a discussion of the Shockley-Queisser limit at Queen Mary University of London, School of Physics and Astronomy, "The Shockley-Queisser Limit," https://ph.qmul.ac.uk/sites/default/files/u75/Solar%20cells_environmental%20impact.pdf. For wind power, see a discussion of the Betz limit, Windpower Program, "The Betz Limit," http://www.wind-power-program.com/betz.htm. There also is the problem of wake effects among wind turbines in a wind farm: The spacing between the turbines must be sufficient to avoid (or to optimize) airflow interference among them. See F. González-Longatt, P. Wall, and V. Terzija, "Wake Effect in Wind Farm Performance: Steady-State and Dynamic Behavior," *Renewable Energy* 39, no. 1 (March 2012): 329–38, https://www.sciencedirect.com/science/article/pii/S0960148111005155. See also endnote 98. The problem of scale diseconomies for wind and solar power at the industry level is discussed below.

74. Crudely, the capacity factor for a given power plant technology is the output that can be expected over the course of, say, a year, divided by the output that would be observed if the technology were producing at full capacity. For example, suppose that a natural gas combined cycle plant with a capacity of 800 MW would produce about seven million mWh (there are 8,760 hours in a year) at full capacity, but instead produces only six million mWh, because of maintenance downtime and the like. The capacity factor would be about 85 percent. In the language of the electricity sector, "dispatchable" is the term corresponding to "predictable." A power source is dispatchable if it can be scheduled reliably; neither wind nor solar power is dispatchable.

75. See Ronald M. Barone and Benjamin Zycher, "The Magnitude of Rooftop Solar Subsidies and Why It Matters," American Enterprise Institute, November 2017, http://www.aei.org/wp-content/uploads/2017/11/

Rooftop-Solar-Subsidies.pdf.

76. See Benjamin Zycher, *Renewable Electricity Generation: Economic Analysis and Outlook* (Washington DC: AEI Press, 2011), 22–31, http://www.aei.org/publication/renewable-electricity-generation. Even if we assume scale economies at the turbine or solar panel level (a larger turbine or solar panel would produce power at a lower average cost) and even if we assume scale economies at the wind farm or utility-scale solar field level (a wind farm with more turbines or a solar field with more heliostats/panels would produce power at a lower average cost), it remains the case that scale diseconomies must result as the renewable power sector expands to additional sites. One circumvention of this problem might be construction of wind facilities offshore—the discussion above assumes the construction of only onshore wind capacity in a GND effort—but that ignores the vastly higher capital costs of offshore wind facilities. EIA estimates capital costs of $1.62 million per MW for onshore wind facilities and $6.54 million per MW for offshore investments. See US Energy Information Administration, "Cost and Performance Characteristics of New Generating Technologies, Annual Energy Outlook 2019," January 2019, 2, Table 2, https://www.eia.gov/outlooks/aeo/assumptions/pdf/table_8.2.pdf.

77. In other words, as the industry expands to ever-more sites, there will be fewer good wind and sunlight days on average, with fewer mWh of generation over which to "spread" large fixed costs.

78. See US Department of Energy, *Maintaining Reliability in the Modern Power System*, December 2016, https://www.energy.gov/sites/prod/files/2017/01/f34/Maintaining%20Reliability%20in%20the%20Modern%20Power%20System.pdf.

79. See, for example, Patricio Rocha-Garrido, "Effective Load Carrying Capability (ELCC) Analysis for Wind and Solar Resources," presentation, PJM, December 10, 2018, https://pjm.com/-/media/committees-groups/subcommittees/irs/20181210/20181210-item-04-wind-solar-effective-load-carrying-capability-elcc.ashx. See also Steve Huntoon (principal, Energy Counsel LLP), in discussion with the author, February 18, 2019.

80. See M. M. Hand et al., *Renewable Electricity Futures Study*, National Renewable Energy Laboratory, 2012, Figure ES-10, https://www.nrel.gov/docs/fy13osti/52409-ES.pdf.

81. See US Energy Information Administration, "Levelized Cost and Levelized Avoided Cost of New Generation Resources in the *Annual Energy Outlook*

2018," March 2018, Table 1a, https://www.eia.gov/outlooks/aeo/pdf/electricity_generation.pdf; US Department of Energy, *2017 Wind Technologies Market Report,* August 2018, Figure 33, https://www.energy.gov/sites/prod/files/2018/08/f54/2017_wind_technologies_market_report_8.15.18.v2.pdf; Lazard, "Lazard's Levelized Cost of Energy Analysis—Version 12.0," 2018, 13 and 15, https://www.lazard.com/media/450784/lazards-levelized-cost-of-energy-version-120-vfinal.pdf; and Thomas F. Stacy and George S. Taylor, *The Levelized Cost of Electricity from Existing Generation Resources,* Institute for Energy Research, July 2016, 25, https://www.instituteforenergyresearch.org/wp-content/uploads/2016/07/IER_LCOE_2016-2.pdf. For coal capacity without carbon capture and sequestration (CCS), the EIA assumed capacity factor is 85 percent. See US Energy Information Administration, *Annual Energy Outlook 2015,* Table A5, https://www.eia.gov/outlooks/aeo/pdf/appendix_tbls.pdf. CCS technology has not been shown to be feasible economically at current price levels for natural gas, even apart from the lack of pipeline or other transport capacity to move "captured" and "sequestered" carbon dioxide to storage sites. See endnote 4.

82. Net summer capacity for these conventional technologies was 864.3 GW in 2007 and 847.9 GW in 2017. See US Energy Information Administration, *Electric Power Annual* (data for 2017), October 22, 2018, Table 4.2.A, https://www.eia.gov/electricity/annual/html/epa_04_03.html.

83. From 2007 to 2017, real GDP grew at an annual compound rate of less than 1.5 percent. See US Bureau of Economic Analysis, National Data, https://apps.bea.gov/iTable/iTable.cfm?reqid=19&step=2#reqid=19&step=2&isuri=1&1921=survey. For electricity generation with the conventional technologies listed above, net generation fell from 3,798.7 tWh in 2007 to 3,341.1 tWh in 2017, in substantial part due to subsidies and mandated market shares for renewable power. Total generation from all utility-scale facilities fell from 4,156.7 tWh in 2007 to 4,034.3 tWh in 2017. See US Energy Information Administration, *Electric Power Annual* (data for 2017), October 22, 2018, Table 3.1.A, https://www.eia.gov/electricity/annual/html/epa_04_03.html.

84. If the capacity factors were equal, then in principle the replacement would be one-to-one—that is, the adjustment factor would be 0.87/0.87 = 1. See US Department of Energy, "Maintaining Reliability in the Modern Power System," December 2016, https://www.energy.gov/sites/prod/files/2017/01/f34/Maintaining%20Reliability%20in%20the%20Modern%20Power%20System.pdf.

85. Tables 3, 5, and 6; US Energy Information Administration, *Electric Power Annual* (data for 2017), October 22, 2018, Tables 3.1.A and 8.4, https://www.eia.gov/electricity/annual/html/epa_04_03.html; and author computations.

86. The aggregate household data are reported by the US Bureau of the Census, Historical Households Tables, Table HH-1, https://www.census.gov/data/tables/time-series/demo/families/households.html.

87. For a more detailed discussion, see Benjamin Zycher, *Renewable Electricity Generation: Economic Analysis and Outlook* (Washington DC: AEI Press, 2011), 22–31, http://www.aei.org/publication/renewable-electricity-generation.

88. The "levelized" costs are the uniform annual costs of a project (or project component) that have the same present value as the actual cost streams.

89. See US Energy Information Administration, "Levelized Cost and Levelized Avoided Cost of New Generation Resources in the Annual Energy Outlook 2018," March 2018, Table 1a, https://www.eia.gov/outlooks/aeo/pdf/electricity_generation.pdf.

90. From Table 3, existing wind and solar capacity is 130.7 GW. From Table 6, wind and solar replacement capacity under the GND would be 2626.8 GW. See Steve Huntoon, "Alternative Facts and Global Warming," *RTO Insider*, August 8, 2017, http://www.energy-counsel.com/docs/Alternative-Facts-and-Global-Warming.pdf.

91. Generation to be replaced (2017 data) is 3,341.1 tWh, with the replacement generation being 2,238.5 tWh of wind power and 1,102.6 tWh of solar power. The additional transmission costs are, respectively, $4.8 million and $6.6 million per tWh for wind and solar. Accordingly, (2238.5 * $4.8 million) + (1102.6 * $6.6 million) = $18 billion.

92. See Table 6 and Chapter 3. Author computations based on US Energy Information Administration, Total Energy, https://www.eia.gov/totalenergy/data/browser/index.php?tbl=T01.01#/?f=M; and US Energy Information Administration, *Electric Power Annual* (data for 2017), October 22, 2018, Table 8.4, https://www.eia.gov/electricity/annual/html/epa_04_03.html. Annual backup generation of 1380.6 tWh was derived as follows: 394 GW of backup capacity (= 15 percent of 2627 GW), capacity factor of 40 percent, 8,760 hours in a year. Computation: 394 * 0.4 * 8760 = 1380.6 tWh.

93. For a discussion, see Executive Office of the President, "Economic Benefits of Increasing Electric Grid Resilience to Weather Outages," August 2013, https://www.energy.gov/sites/prod/files/2013/08/f2/Grid%20Resiliency%20

Report_FINAL.pdf. See also Joseph H. Eto, "The National Cost of Power Interruptions to Electricity Customers," presentation, Institute of Electrical and Electronics Engineers, http://grouper.ieee.org/groups/td/dist/sd/doc/2016-09-02%20LBNL%202016%20Updated%20Estimate-Nat%20Cost%20of%20Pwr%20Interruptions%20to%20Elec%20Custs-Joe%20Eto.pdf.

94. See Steve Huntoon, "Battery Storage: Drinking the Electric Kool-Aid," *Public Utilities Fortnightly* 154, no. 1 (January 2016): 36–45 and 52, http://www.energy-counsel.com/docs/Battery-Storage-Drinking-the-Electric-Kool-Aid-Fortnightly-January-2016.pdf. See also Jack Ponton, "Grid-Scale Storage: Can It Solve the Intermittency Problem?," Global Warming Policy Foundation, 2018, https://www.thegwpf.org/content/uploads/2019/02/GridStorageWeb-1.pdf; and Robert Blohm, "The Green New Deal's Impossible Electric Grid," *Wall Street Journal*, February 20, 2019, https://www.wsj.com/articles/the-green-new-deals-impossible-electric-grid-11550705997.

95. The PJM Interconnection is a regional transmission organization (RTO) that coordinates the movement of wholesale electricity in all or parts of Delaware, Illinois, Indiana, Kentucky, Maryland, Michigan, New Jersey, North Carolina, Ohio, Pennsylvania, Tennessee, Virginia, West Virginia, and the District of Columbia. See PJM, https://www.pjm.com/.

96. See Vaclav Smil, *Energy at the Crossroads* (Cambridge, MA: MIT Press, 2003), 276–78. Energy concentration in simple terms is the energy content of a given fuel per volume. Peter Huber and Mark Mills note that coal supplies about twice as much energy as wood on a pound-for-pound basis, while oil provides about twice as much as coal, and a gram of uranium 235 has as much energy as four tons of coal. See also Peter W. Huber and Mark P. Mills, *The Bottomless Well: The Twilight of Fuel, the Virtue of Waste, and Why We Will Never Run out of Energy* (New York: Basic Books, 2005), 8.

97. Note that the average nameplate capacity of wind turbines installed in the US in 2017 was 2.32 MW, an increase of 8 percent from 2016. See US Department of Energy, *2017 Wind Technologies Market Report*, August 2018, viii, https://www.energy.gov/sites/prod/files/2018/08/f54/2017_wind_technologies_market_report_8.15.18.v2.pdf. The figures for 2007, 2008, and 2009 were, respectively, 1.65 MW, 1.66 MW, and 1.74 MW. See US Department of Energy, "2009 Wind Technologies Market Report," August 2010, v, http://www1.eere.energy.gov/windandhydro/pdfs/2009_wind_technologies_market_report.pdf.

98. Wake effects are interferences with wind speeds for a given turbine

caused by other turbines in a wind farm. The usual assumed spacing requirement is 5–10 turbine diameters apart. In 2017, 99 percent of newly installed
wind turbines had rotor diameters at least 100 meters, 80 percent had rotor
diameters over 110 meters, and 14 percent were at least 120 meters. See US
Department of Energy, 2017 *Wind Technologies Market Report*, ix. Smil discusses
turbine spacing requirements and theoretical limits on the amount of energy
that can be extracted from wind flows. Vaclav Smil, *Energy at the Crossroads*
(Cambridge, MA: MIT Press, 2003), 276. See also endnote 73. There is little
dissent in the literature from the proposition that the energy content of wind
flows is highly diffuse. Note that the energy content of wind increases with
the cube of the change in wind speed, so that a doubling of the latter increases
the former by a factor of eight. As a rough generalization, wind turbines begin
to produce power when wind speeds reach about 5 mph, reach rated capacity
at about 30–35 mph, and are designed to shut down at about 50–55 mph to
prevent damage from storms.

99. Some of the land used by wind farms but not actually bearing turbines,
other equipment, or access roads might remain available for farming or other
purposes. Such considerations are highly site specific, and no systematic data
on this issue seem to be available. For a skeptical discussion, see Robert Bryce,
Power Hungry: The Myths of "Green" Energy and the Real Fuels of the Future (New
York: Public Affairs, 2010), 84–85.

100. See Landon Stevens et al., *The Footprint of Energy: Land Use of U.S.
Electricity Production*, STRATA, June 2017, https://www.strata.org/pdf/2017/
footprints-full.pdf.

101. Solar radiation at the top of the atmosphere perpendicular to the earth
is 1360 W/m2. Because half the earth is dark at any given time and because
not all sunlight is perpendicular to the earth, average effective solar radiation
at the top of the atmosphere is one-quarter of that, or 340 W/m2. Because of
albedo effects (reflection of sunlight back into space by clouds, ice masses,
deserts, and the like), average solar radiation at the surface is about 240 W/m2.
See NASA Earth Observatory, "Incoming Sunlight," January 14, 2009, https://
earthobservatory.nasa.gov/features/EnergyBalance/page2.php. See also Benjamin Zycher, "California's New Solar Plant: Burning Up Taxpayer Money,
Land, and Wildlife," *American*, May 21, 2014, http://www.aei.org/publication/
californias-new-solar-plant-burning-up-taxpayer-money-land-and-wildlife/.

102. See Zycher, "California's New Solar Plant."

103. See Paul Denholm et al., *Land-Use Requirements of Modern Wind Power Plants in the United States*, National Renewable Energy Laboratory, August 2009, Table 1, https://www.nrel.gov/docs/fy09osti/45834.pdf; and Sean Ong et al., *Land-Use Requirements for Solar Power Plants in the United States*, National Renewable Energy Laboratory, June 2013, Table ES-1, https://www.nrel.gov/docs/fy13osti/56290.pdf.

104. See US Census Bureau, "State Area Measurements and Internal Point Coordinates," https://www.census.gov/geo/reference/state-area.html.

105. See US Department of Agriculture, *Land Values: 2017 Summary*, August 2017, https://www.usda.gov/nass/PUBS/TODAYRPT/land0817.pdf.

106. See the 2017 price data reported in US Energy Information Administration, "State Electricity Profiles," January 8, 2019, https://www.eia.gov/electricity/state/. Note that the 2017 average price of power ($104.80 per mWh) implicitly includes the economic cost of emissions, in that the costs of required equipment for the control of emissions is reflected in the price. This assumes that regulations controlling such emissions yield an approximate balancing of the marginal benefits and costs of emissions reductions. The same would be true for the equipment required for the backup units, but the same is not true for the environmental effects of wind and solar power, adverse but unregulated. See the discussion in Chapter 3.

107. The after-tax household income data by income quintile reported by the Bureau of Labor Statistics can be found in US Bureau of Labor Statistics, BLS Data Finder 1.1, s.v. "Income Quintiles," https://beta.bls.gov/dataQuery/find?st=400&r=100&s=title%3AA&q=income+quintiles&more=0.

108. See Paul L. Joskow, "Comparing the Costs of Intermittent and Dispatchable Electricity Generating Technologies," *American Economic Review* 101, no. 3 (May 2011): 238–41.

109. This problem is not relevant for comparisons of dispatchable generation technologies (e.g., coal versus natural gas) because the values of the electricity produced by dispatchable units are more or less the same, except for units designed to operate predominantly at periods of peak demand. An example of such units are gas turbines.

110. See Tyler Cowen, "Public Goods and Externalities," in *The Concise Encyclopedia of Economics*, ed. David Henderson (Indianapolis, IN: Library of Economics and Liberty, 2002), http://www.econlib.org/library/Enc1/PublicGoodsandExternalities.html.

111. See, for example, Iain Murray, "Economics of Green New Deal: More Red Than Green," Competitive Enterprise Institute, February 14, 2019, https://cei. org/blog/economics-green-new-deal-more-red-green; William L. Anderson, "AOC's Green New Deal Is a U.S. Version of Mao's Disastrous Great Leap Forward," Foundation for Economic Education, February 12, 2019, https://fee.org/ articles/aocs-green-new-deal-is-a-us-version-of-mao-s-disastrous-great-leap-forward/; Jason Pye, "The Green New Deal Is Communist Manifesto, 21st Century," RealClearMarkets, February 9, 2019, https://www.realclearmarkets.com/ articles/2019/02/09/the_green_new_deal_is_communist_manifesto_21st_century_103617.html; and David French, "The Green New Deal Is Everything That's Wrong with Progressive Environmentalism," *National Review*, February 7, 2019, https://www.nationalreview.com/2019/02/green-new-deal-is-everything-thats-wrong-with-progressive-environmentalism/.

112. For contrary arguments on the private provision of public goods, see C. M. Lindsay and William R. Dougan, "Efficiency in the Provision of Pure Public Goods by Private Citizens," *Public Choice* 156, no. 1/2 (July 2013): 31–43, https://www.jstor.org/stable/42003145?seq=1#page_scan_tab_contents; Harold Demsetz, "The Private Production of Public Goods," *Journal of Law & Economics* 13, no. 2 (October 1970): 293–306, https://www.jstor.org/stable/725027; and Earl A. Thompson, "The Perfectly Competitive Production of Collective Goods," *Review of Economics and Statistics* 50, no. 1 (February 1968): 1–12, https://www.jstor.org/stable/1927051.

113. For the pure private good, consumption of a unit of the good (e.g., an apple) by one individual means that that unit is no longer available to other individuals. And those refusing to pay for apples can be prevented from consuming them. For a collective good (e.g., national defense), consumption of a unit of the resulting protection from foreign threats can be enjoyed by a given individual without reducing the quantity available for other individuals, and those not paying their taxes cannot be excluded from consuming that protection.

114. This is just the simple prediction from standard economic theory that the consumption basket that maximizes well-being ("utility") is the one at which the aggregated preferences and the budget constraint have the same slope, –1 in our example.

115. I ignore here the possibility of side payments, a topic closely related to the analysis of congressional bargaining. See Bryan Ellickson, "A Generalization

of the Pure Theory of Public Goods," *American Economic Review* 63, no. 3 (June 1973): 417–32.

116. See James M. Buchanan, *Demand and Supply of Public Goods* (Chicago: Rand McNally, 1968), 77–125; and Bryan Ellickson, "A Generalization of the Pure Theory of Public Goods," *American Economic Review* 63, no. 3 (June 1973): 417–32.

117. See Charles Blahous, "The Costs of a National Single-Payer Healthcare System" (working paper, Mercatus Center, July 2018), https://www.mercatus. org/system/files/blahous-costs-medicare-mercatus-working-paper-v1_1. pdf; John Holahan et al., "The Sanders Single-Payer Health Care Plan: The Effect on National Health Expenditures and Federal and Private Spending," Urban Institute, May 9, 2016, https://www.urban.org/research/publication/ sanders-single-payer-health-care-plan-effect-national-health-expenditures- and-federal-and-private-spending; Mark Paul, William Darity Jr., and Darrick Hamilton, "The Federal Job Guarantee—a Policy to Achieve Permanent Full Employment," Center on Budget and Policy Priorities, March 9, 2018, https://www.cbpp.org/research/full-employment/the-federal-job-guarantee-a- policy-to-achieve-permanent-full-employment; Gordon Mermin, Len Burman, and Frank Sammartino, "An Analysis of Senator Bernie Sanders's Tax and Transfer Proposals," Tax Policy Center, May 9, 2016, https://www. taxpolicycenter.org/sites/default/files/alfresco/publication-pdfs/2000786- an-analysis-of-senator-bernie-sanderss-tax-and-transfer-proposals.pdf; and Douglas Holtz-Eakin et al., "The Green New Deal: Scope, Scale, and Implications," American Action Forum, February 25, 2019, https://www. americanactionforum.org/research/the-green-new-deal-scope-scale-and- implications/.

118. Note that H.R. 109, 10–11, mandates that the federal government provide "adequate capital" for the GND "goals and mobilization."

119. Strictly speaking, the excess burden (or "deadweight loss") is the difference between aggregate output under the existing tax system and aggregate output under a different system of "lump-sum" taxes that would yield the same revenues without distorting economic activity. Because government output is not worthless, a zero-tax, zero-outlay, zero-excess burden environment in principle might yield aggregate output lower than that observed under the existing tax system even though, again, the excess burden of taxation would be zero.

120. My AEI colleague Alan Viard in a private communication points out that

"marginal excess burden varies across revenue sources and is not really that well defined." It is "probably more useful to talk about the efficiency cost of redistribution." Alan D. Viard (resident scholar, American Enterprise Institute), in discussion with the author, February 15, 2019.

121. Martin A. Feldstein, "The Effect of Taxes on Efficiency and Growth," *Tax Notes*, May 8, 2006, 679–84.

122. See Jason J. Fichtner and Jacob M. Feldman, "The Hidden Cost of Federal Tax Policy," Mercatus Center, 2015, Table 1.3, https://www.mercatus.org/system/files/fichtner_hidden_cost_ch1_web.pdf.

123. See Stephanie Kelton, Andres Bernal, and Greg Carlock, "We Can Pay for a Green New Deal," Huffington Post, November 30, 2018, https://www.huffingtonpost.com/entry/opinion-green-new-deal-cost_us_5c0042b2e4b027f1097bda5b. For a video exposition in defense of borrowing financed with money creation, see Stephanie Kelton, "The Public Purse," video, Sanders Institute, https://www.sandersinstitute.com/blog/the-public-purse. For a history of inflationary finance, see Peter Bernholz, *Monetary Regimes and Inflation: History, Economic and Political Relationships*, 2nd ed. (Cheltenham, UK: Edward Elgar, 2015).

124. For useful critiques, see Stan Veuger, "Modern Monetary Theory and Policy," AEI Economic Perspectives, January 2019, https://www.aei.org/wp-content/uploads/2019/01/Modern-Monetary-Theory-and-Policy.pdf; and Michael R. Strain, "'Modern Monetary Theory' Is a Joke That's Not Funny," Bloomberg Opinion, January 17, 2019, https://www.bloomberg.com/opinion/articles/2019-01-17/modern-monetary-theory-would-sink-u-s-in-debt. See also Thomas I. Palley, "The Critics of Modern Monetary Theory (MMT) Are Right," *Review of Political Economy* 27, no. 1 (2015): 45–61, https://www.tandfonline.com/doi/abs/10.1080/09538259.2014.957473?src=recsys&journalCode=crpe20; and Lawrence H. Summers, "The Left's Embrace of Modern Monetary Theory Is a Recipe for Disaster," *Washington Post*, March 4, 2019.

125. On the problem of capturing the quasi-rents created by the existence of large illiquid (or "non-salvageable") capital investments—the general case that includes an attempt to renege on the repayment of real debt—see Benjamin Klein and Keith B. Leffler, "The Role of Market Forces in Assuring Contractual Performance," *Journal of Political Economy* 89, no. 4 (August 1981): 615–41, https://www.jstor.org/stable/1833028?seq=1#page_scan_tab_contents. In principle, a government interested in preserving its future ability to borrow

at reasonable rates, or at all, may have incentives to preserve the credibility of its repayment promises. But that dynamic may not constrain fully the behavior of current policymakers interested in acquiring resources for current spending purposes; the adverse effects of imposing real losses on creditors would be inflicted upon their successors in office. Whether the incentives of long-lived political parties serve to limit such behavior is an open question.

126. Consider the standard quantity equation of exchange: $MV = PT$; that is, money times velocity equals nominal income (prices times transactions). This is not merely an equilibrium condition; it is an identity, that is, always true. An increase in M and thus P (inflation) cannot reduce velocity in that an increase in inflation would induce holders of non-interest-bearing money to spend it ever faster to avoid further losses in real purchasing power.

127. See the discussion above of the cost of government provision of a collective good under a majority decision rule. For a classic discussion of inflation, see Reuben A. Kessel and Armen A. Alchian, "Effects of Inflation," *Journal of Political Economy* 70, no. 6 (December 1962): 521–37, https://www.jstor.org/stable/1828777. See also Armen A. Alchian and William R. Allen, *Universal Economics*, ed. Jerry L. Jordan (Carmel, IN: Liberty Fund, 2018), 657–80.

128. For an elaboration of this point, see Stan Veuger, "Modern Monetary Theory and Policy," AEI Economic Perspectives, January 2019, https://www.aei.org/wp-content/uploads/2019/01/Modern-Monetary-Theory-and-Policy.pdf.

129. See the data reported by the Federal Reserve Bank of St. Louis, FRED, s.v. "Currency in Circulation," https://fred.stlouisfed.org/series/WCURCIR.

130. See Richard G. Anderson, "Inflation's Economic Cost: How Large? How Certain?," Federal Reserve Bank of St. Louis, July 2006, https://www.stlouisfed.org/publications/regional-economist/july-2006/inflations-economic-cost-how-large-how-certain.

131. See *Duquesne Light Co. v. Barasch*, 488 U.S. 299 (1989), https://supreme.justia.com/cases/federal/us/488/299/. For a useful discussion, see Sean P. Madden, "Takings Clause Analysis of Utility Ratemaking Decisions: Measuring Hope's Investor Interest Factor," *Fordham Law Review* 58, no. 3 (1989): 427–46. On the issue of public-utility investments deemed prudent by regulatory authorities, see Benjamin Zycher, "Economic Efficiency and 'Prudence' Analysis of Power Plant Investment," *Contemporary Economic Policy* 6, no. 3 (July 1988): 42–59, https://onlinelibrary.wiley.com/doi/pdf/10.1111/

j.1465-7287.1988.tb00292.x.

132. See Richard Seager et al., *Causes and Predictability of the 2011–14 California Drought*, National Oceanographic and Atmospheric Administration, December 2014, https://cpo.noaa.gov/Meet-the-Divisions/Earth-System-Science-and-Modeling/MAPP/MAPP-Task-Forces/Drought/Drought-Task-Force-I/Causes-and-Predictability-of-the-2011-2014-California-Drought. For the recent precipitation data for California, see National Oceanic and Atmospheric Administration, "Monthly Precipitation Summary Water Year 2019," https://www.cnrfc.noaa.gov/monthly_precip.php.

133. See, for example, Gary D. Libecap, "The Problem of Water," *Regulation* 37, no. 3 (Fall 2014), https://object.cato.org/sites/cato.org/files/serials/files/regulation/2014/10/regulationv37n3-9_1.pdf#page=7.

134. See Taryn Luna and Alexei Koseff, "Get Ready to Save Water: Permanent California Restrictions Approved by Gov. Brown," *Sacramento Bee*, May 31, 2018, https://www.sacbee.com/news/politics-government/capitol-alert/article211333594.html. Details of the legislation are summarized in a California Water Boards fact sheet: California Water Boards, "Water Efficiency Legislation Will Make California More Resilient to Impacts of Future Droughts," June 7, 2018, https://www.waterboards.ca.gov/publications_forms/publications/factsheets/docs/water_efficiency_bill_factsheet.pdf. See also Jarrett Stepman, "Blame California's Crazy Left-Wing Politics for Water Rationing," Daily Signal, June 6, 2018, https://www.dailysignal.com/2018/06/06/blame-californias-crazy-left-wing-politics-for-water-rationing/.

135. See US Department of Energy, "What Is the Smart Grid?," https://www.smartgrid.gov/the_smart_grid/smart_grid.html.

136. See Smart Energy Consumer Collaborative, "Smart Meters," http://www.whatissmartgrid.org/smart-grid-101/smart-meters.

137. See H.R. 109, 9.

138. See, for example, Loren E. Lomasky, "Autonomy and Automobility," *Independent Review* 2, no. 1 (Summer 1997): 5–28, http://www.independent.org/pdf/tir/tir_02_1_lomasky.pdf.

139. The GND framework recognizes the adverse transitional employment implications of a massive transformation of the US energy, transportation, and physical plant/building infrastructure and so proposes an equally massive employment program, with a federal job guarantee, a topic not addressed here directly.

140. Considerable employment would be created if policies encouraged ditch-digging with shovels (or, in Milton Friedman's famous example, spoons) rather than heavy equipment. Such employment obviously would be laughable—that is, an obvious economic burden. There is no analytic difference between this example and the "green jobs" rationale for renewables policies.

141. See the discussion in endnote 15 of individual preferences as the source of "value." Many advocates of renewables subsidies assert that solar and wind power is more labor intensive than conventional generation. The assumption of greater labor intensity for renewable power production is dubious: The operation of solar or wind facilities does not employ large amounts of labor, and it is far from clear that construction of solar or wind facilities is more labor intensive than construction of conventional generation facilities.

142. It is important to keep clear the conceptual experiment under consideration. In the context here, I assume that government policies increase the substitution of renewable power in place of conventional electricity and ask whether the aggregate data are consistent with the assertion that such "green" policies—explicitly an increase in energy costs—can be predicted to yield an increase in aggregate employment. This is very different from, say, the effects of an aggregate recession, which can be predicted to reduce both energy costs (prices) and employment more or less simultaneously. Similarly, an economic boom would increase both energy prices and employment, while an increase in energy supplies would reduce energy prices and increase employment. Note that aggregate employment in any of these scenarios might fall in the short run as market forces reallocate labor (and other resources) in response to changes in relative prices.

143. Note that greater energy "efficiency" in any given activity can yield an increase in actual energy consumption, if the elasticity of energy demand with respect to the marginal cost of energy use is greater than one. If, for example, air conditioning were to become sufficiently "efficient" in terms of energy consumption per degree of cooling, it is possible that air conditioners would be run so much—or that so many additional air conditioners would be installed—that total energy consumption in space cooling would increase.

144. H.R. 109 refers to "sustainability" in various contexts four times in 14 pages. There is considerable discussion in the technical literature of nonbiological sources of methane and petroleum. See James A. Kent, *Kent and Riegel's Handbook of Industrial Chemistry and Biotechnology*, 11th ed. (New York: Springer,

2007), chap. 20; and M. Ragheb, "Biogenic and Abiogenic Petroleum," January 6, 2019, http://mragheb.com/NPRE%20402%20ME%20405%20Nuclear%20 Power%20Engineering/Biogenic%20and%20Abiogenic%20Petroleum.pdf. To the extent that conventional energy resources are produced nonbiologically, the "depletion" assumption underlying the sustainability argument may be incorrect even descriptively.

145. See US Environmental Protection Agency, "Learn About Sustainability," October 18, 2016, https://www.epa.gov/sustainability/learn-about-sustainability#what.

146. See United Nations, *Report of the World Commission on Environment and Development: Our Common Future*, para. 27, http://www.un-documents.net/ our-common-future.pdf.

147. In reality the long-run prices of most exhaustible natural resources have declined (after adjusting for inflation), largely because of (unexpected) technological advances in discovery, production, and use. See Julian L. Simon, *The Ultimate Resource 2* (Princeton, NJ: Princeton University Press, 1996).

148. Strictly speaking, it is not the price of the resource that should rise at the market rate of interest; instead the total economic return to holding the resource for future use should equal the market rate of interest. That total economic return includes expected price changes and capital gains, expected cost savings, and the like. Current and expected prices are a reasonable first approximation of (or proxy for) that total economic return.

149. For a more detailed conceptual and empirical discussion of the market allocation of a depletable resource over time, see Benjamin Zycher, "World Oil Prices: Market Expectations, the House of Saud, and the Transient Effect of Supply Disruptions," American Enterprise Institute, June 2016, http://www.aei. org/wp-content/uploads/2016/06/World-Oil-Prices.pdf.

150. See Barack Obama, *Economic Report of the President*, January 2017, 440, https://obamawhitehouse.archives.gov/sites/default/files/docs/2017_ economic_report_of_president.pdf.

151. Gail Kennedy (professor, Department of Anthropology, University of California, Los Angeles), in discussion with the author, February 6, 2011. Note here again the implicit normative assumption that the "interests" of any individual or group are those that they would define for themselves or, more important, reveal through choice behavior. See endnote 15.

152. The capital stock includes both tangible capital and such intangibles as

the rule of law, the stock of knowledge, culture, and the like. Greater wealth for the current generation yielded by resource consumption yields conditions allowing the expansion of other dimensions of the capital stock defined broadly.

153. Arnold C. Harberger and Glenn P. Jenkins, "Musings on the Social Discount Rate," *Journal of Benefit-Cost Analysis* 6, no. 1 (Spring 2015): 6–32, https://www.cambridge.org/core/journals/journal-of-benefit-cost-analysis/article/musings-on-the-social-discount-rate-1/37937B05472F0E72436BC1FDB068C5D5.

154. James Broughel, "The Social Discount Rate: A Baseline Approach" (working paper, Mercatus Center, January 2017), https://www.mercatus.org/system/files/mercatus-broughel-social-discount-rate-v1.pdf.

155. Robert S. Pindyck, "Climate Change Policy: What Do the Models Tell Us?," *Journal of Economic Literature* 51, no. 3 (September 2013): 860–72, https://pubs.aeaweb.org/doi/pdfplus/10.1257/jel.51.3.860.

156. Juzhong Zhuang et al., "Theory and Practice in the Choice of Social Discount Rate for Cost-Benefit Analysis: A Survey," Asian Development Bank, May 2007, https://www.adb.org/sites/default/files/publication/28360/wp094.pdf.

157. See Kenneth J. Arrow et al., "Should Government Use a Declining Discount Rate in Project Analysis?," *Review of Environmental Economics and Policy* 8, no. 2 (Summer 2014): 145–63, https://academic.oup.com/reep/article/8/2/145/2888825.

158. See Climate Research Unit of East Anglia University, "Temperature," January 2016, https://crudata.uea.ac.uk/cru/data/temperature/HadCRUT4.pdf. On the Little Ice Age, see Michael E. Mann, "Little Ice Age," in *Encyclopedia of Global Environmental Change, Volume 1: The Earth System: Physical and Chemical Dimensions of Global Environmental Change*, ed. Michael C. MacCracken and John S. Perry (Chichester, UK: John Wiley & Sons, 2002), http://www.meteo.psu.edu/holocene/public_html/shared/articles/littleiceage.pdf. On the evidence of anthropogenic effects, see John R. Christy and Richard T. McNider, "Satellite Bulk Tropospheric Temperatures as a Metric for Climate Sensitivity," *Asia-Pacific Journal of Atmospheric Science* 53, no. 4 (2017): 511–18, https://wattsupwiththat.files.wordpress.com/2017/11/2017_christy_mcnider-1.pdf; and Nicholas Lewis and Judith Curry, "The Impact of Recent Forcing and Ocean Heat Uptake Data on Estimates of Climate Sensitivity," *Journal of Climate* 31, no. 15 (August 2018): 6051–71, https://journals.ametsoc.org/doi/abs/10.1175/

JCLI-D-17-0667.1. On the reality of anthropogenic warming, see University of Alabama, Huntsville, "UAH Version 6.0 Global Average Temperature Variations for 4 Atmospheric Layers," http://www.drroyspencer.com/wp-content/uploads/version6-msu234-global-anomaly-time-series.gif. Note, however, that the absence of a trend for lower stratosphere temperatures since approximately the mid-1990s suggests that the recent "pause" in temperature increases is not the result of measurement error.

159. See Judith Curry, *Sea Level and Climate Change*, Climate Forecast Applications Network, November 25, 2018, 9–34, https://curryja.files.wordpress.com/2018/11/special-report-sea-level-rise3.pdf.

160. See the data reported by National Oceanic and Atmospheric Administration, National Centers for Environmental Information, "Sea Ice and Snow Cover Extent," https://www.ncdc.noaa.gov/snow-and-ice/extent/sea-ice/N/0.

161. See the data reported by National Oceanic and Atmospheric Administration, National Centers for Environmental Information, "Historical Records and Trends," https://www.ncdc.noaa.gov/climate-information/extreme-events/us-tornado-climatology/trends.

162. See the satellite data on cyclone frequencies and accumulated energy reported in Ryan N. Maue, "Global Tropical Cyclone Activity," http://policlimate.com/tropical/.

163. See the wildfire data reported by the National Interagency Fire Center at National Interagency Fire Center, "Total Wildland Fires and Acres (1926–2017)," https://www.nifc.gov/fireInfo/fireInfo_stats_totalFires.html.

164. Staff, California Forestry Association and the California Department of Forestry and Fire Protection, in discussion with the author, November 2018.

165. On drought conditions, see the time-series data for the Palmer Drought Severity Index reported in US Environmental Protection Agency, "Climate Change Indicators: Drought," https://www.epa.gov/climate-indicators/climate-change-indicators-drought. On the correlation between US flooding and atmospheric GHG concentrations, see R. M. Hirsch and K. R. Ryberg, "Has the Magnitude of Floods Across the USA Changed with Global CO_2 Levels?," *Hydrological Sciences Journal* 57, no. 1 (2012): 1–9, https://www.tandfonline.com/doi/full/10.1080/02626667.2011.621895.

166. The most comprehensive data reported on ocean acidification issues is the Ocean Acidification Database. Center for the Study of Carbon Dioxide and Global Change, "Ocean Acidification Database," http://www.co2science.org/

data/acidification/results.php. See also Alan Longhurst, *Doubt and Certainty in Climate Science*, March 2012–September 2015, 214–25, https://curryja.files.wordpress.com/2015/09/longhurst-print.pdf.

167. See Matthew Collins et al., "Long-Term Climate Change: Projections, Commitments, and Irreversibility," in *Climate Change 2013: The Physical Science*, ed. Thomas F. Stocker et al. (Cambridge, UK: Cambridge University Press, 2013), Table 12.4, https://www.ipcc.ch/site/assets/uploads/2018/02/WG1AR5_Chapter12_FINAL.pdf.

168. For a discussion of the policy implications of the four IPCC representative concentration pathways, see Benjamin Zycher, "The Climate Empire Strikes Out: The Perils of Policy Analysis in an Echo Chamber," American Enterprise Institute, September 26, 2018, https://www.aei.org/publication/the-climate-empire-strikes-out-the-perils-of-policy-analysis-in-an-echo-chamber. See also Benjamin Zycher, "Hearken Sinners: The End Is Near," American Enterprise Institute, October 22, 2018, http://www.aei.org/publication/hearken-sinners-the-end-is-near/.

169. Details of the legislation can be found at Green Energy and Green Economy Act, S.O. 2009, https://www.ontario.ca/laws/statute/S09012.

170. Ross R. McKitrick, *Environmental and Economic Consequences of Ontario's Green Energy Act*, Fraser Institute Centre for Energy and Natural Resource Studies, April 11, 2013, https://www.fraserinstitute.org/sites/default/files/environmental-and-economic-consequences-ontarios-green-energy-act.pdf.

171. See Bioenergy International, "Ontario Repeals the Green Energy Act," December 11, 2018, https://bioenergyinternational.com/policy/ontario-repeals-the-green-energy-act.

172. See the cost estimates reported by Douglas Holtz-Eakin et al., "The Green New Deal: Scope, Scale, and Implications," American Action Forum, February 25, 2019, https://www.americanactionforum.org/research/the-green-new-deal-scope-scale-and-implications. Their 10-year cost estimates are $5.4 trillion for the electricity portion of the GND, $1.3–$2.7 trillion for the high-speed rail portion, $6.8–$44.6 trillion for the employment guarantee, $36 trillion for the universal health care portion, $1.6–$4.2 trillion for the housing guarantee and buildings retrofit, and $1.5 billion for the food security portion.

About the Author

Benjamin Zycher (benjamin.zycher@aei.org) is a resident scholar at the American Enterprise Institute (AEI), where he works on energy and environmental policy. He is also a senior fellow at the Pacific Research Institute. Before joining AEI, Zycher conducted a broad research program in his public policy research firm and was an intelligence community associate of the Office of Economic Analysis in the US Department of State's Bureau of Intelligence and Research. He is a former senior economist at the RAND Corporation; a former adjunct professor of economics at the University of California, Los Angeles, (UCLA) and at the California State University Channel Islands; and a former senior economist at the Jet Propulsion Laboratory, California Institute of Technology. He served as a senior staff economist for the President's Council of Economic Advisers, with responsibility for energy and environmental policy issues. Zycher has a doctorate in economics from UCLA; a master's in public policy from the University of California, Berkeley; and a bachelor of arts in political science from UCLA.

Acknowledgments

I thank Robert J. Barro, Don Boudreaux, Richard J. Buddin, Michael Canes, Carl Dahlman, Veronique de Rugy, Chuck DeVore, Laurence A. Dougharty, Myron Ebell, Larry D. Hamlin, William F. Hederman, Steve Huntoon, Omotunde E. G. Johnson, Jerry L. Jordan, Roslyn Layton, Marlo Lewis, Roger E. Meiners, Todd Myers, Don Norman, William Poole, Simon Serfaty, James A. Snyder, Michael R. Strain, and Stan A. Veuger for useful suggestions, but any remaining errors are my responsibility. I thank as well Yisehak Abraham for excellent research assistance.

43450623R00066